Youth Sport and the Law

D1616979

Youth Sport and the Law

A Guide to Legal Issues

written by
Tom Appenzeller

edited by
Herb Appenzeller

Carolina Academic Press
Durham, North Carolina

Library of Congress Cataloging-in-Publication Data

Appenzeller, Thomas.
    Youth sport and the law : a guide to legal issues / written by Tom
Appenzeller ; edited by Herb Appenzeller.
        p.   cm.
    Includes bibliographical references and index.
    ISBN 9-89089-663-1
    1. Sports—Law and legislation—United States. 2. Sports injuries
in children—Law and legislation—United States. 3. Liability for
sports accidents—United States. I. Appenzeller, Herb. II. Title.

KF3989.A965 2000
344.73'099—dc21   99-088424

Carolina Academic Press
700 Kent Street
Durham, North Carolina 27701
Telephone (919) 489-7486
Fax (919) 493-5668
E-mail: cap@cap-press.com
www.cap-press.com

Printed in the United States of America.

Dedicated to my Mother and Father,
the two best parents that a son could have.

Contents

Foreword

They say the apple doesn't fall far from the tree. In my experience, this old adage takes on new meaning as my son, Tom, has chosen a career in sport management, risk management, sport law, teaching, and coaching. He has developed an interest in and passion for youth sport and has put his time and effort in this area of sport. He was an avid participant in youth sport activities that included baseball, basketball, football, track, and wrestling. Since his early days as a youth sport participant, he added coaching, teaching, officiating, and the administration of youth sport programs. He has had the opportunity as a parent to see youth sport from still another side as his son and daughter actively participate in tennis, soccer, cheerleading, and cross country running. This background in youth sport has prepared him for the field of youth sport and along with his legal background in sport law, the ability and background to write about youth sport and the law.

Today there is an unprecedented interest in youth sport and this all-time high rate of participation is accompanied by a record number of sport-related lawsuits. *Youth Sport and the Law* uses actual court cases to gain the attention of the reader to the type of court cases that come before the bar that relates to youth sport. The examples of sport-related litigation provides valuable information to all who participate in youth sport—the participant, administrator, coach, and official. *Youth Sport and the Law* is written in an easy to read style that is legally sound but devoid of burdensome legalese. Judicial decisions are important for the guidelines they provide to all who participate in the youth sport endeavor.

I am pleased that Carolina Academic Press has added the book to its outstanding series in sport law. *Youth Sport and the Law* should be a valuable asset to the series and provide a much needed resource for the millions who are a part of youth sport on the national and international level. The book provides guidelines and recommendations which will greatly improve sport for all concerned.

Herb Appenzeller
Jefferson-Pilot Professor of Sport Management Emeritus
Guilford College, Greensboro, North Carolina

Acknowledgments

I would like to acknowledge two very special people who were instrumental in the publication of this book. First, Herb Appenzeller, editor, father and role model. In 1970 my father wrote the first book in what we now refer to as the discipline of Sports Law. *From the Gym to the Jury* was a landmark, and my father was an early pioneer in trying to make sports and physical education a safer and better experience for everybody. His influence and unyielding support of my professional development is a primary reason for this publication. The second person I would like to recognize is Jeanne Swanson who translated all of my long hand and converted it into manuscript form. Jeanne worked tirelessly and went above and beyond the call of duty in helping make this book a reality. Not only did she do all the typing at night and on weekends after her other responsibilities as Director of the Wingate University Bookstore had been fulfilled, but Jeanne, like my father, has been a true friend over the years. Without these two individuals this book would not have been possible.

Thank you.

Credits

I would like to thank Gil B. Fried, Esq. for contributing Chapter 11, "Sexual Abuse in Youth Sport" to the book. Gil is an Associate Professor at the University of New Haven's School of Business and has written an excellent and timely chapter on one of the dark secrets and dangers of Youth Sport.

I would like to acknowledge and thank Dr. Jerald Hawkins, Director of Sports Medicine at Lander University in Greenwood, South Carolina for his contributions to Chapter 12, "Sports Medicine." In 1984 Dr. Hawkins published *Sports Medicine: A Guide for Youth Sports Coaches* which is an excellent publication regarding the medical aspects of Youth Sports. His chapter on "General Injury Management" written by Dr. Stanley Grosshandler was so thorough and complete on injury care that it served as the foundation for Chapter 12.

I would also like to give credit to the various authors who contributed the stories for "After the Facts." These articles were collected over the last 10 years because of their relationship to Youth Sport. The complete reference to each article is listed at the end of the chapter where it appears.

I would also like to thank Mr. David Sherwood and the Wingate University Sports Information Department for a number of the photographs used in the book.

I would also like to thank Mary Somers for allowing use of several photographs for the book. In Chapter 9, "Persons with Disabilities," all photographs courtesy of *Palaestra*: page 118, F. Schack, *Palaestra*, 15(1), 25; page 119, L. Lieberman, *Palaestra*, 14(1), 30; page 123, F. Schack, Palaestra, 15(1), 21; page 125, C. Stopka, *Palaestra*, 12(2), 29; and page 128, The National Ability Center, *Palaestra*, 10(4), 56.

Youth Sport and the Law

Introduction

It was the summer of 1982, Ronald Reagan was president, the Soviet Union was a world power, and a young boy from rural New Jersey was living his dream. That 10-year-old boy from Runnemeade, New Jersey was playing Little League baseball, and he loved it. To be a Little Leaguer, to wear the big league style uniform, playing under the lights on manicured fields, what else is there in the spring and summer for a young boy to do. In rural America, Little League baseball is hot dogs, apple pie, and Mom all rolled into one. Not only was the young athlete living his dream, he was a good baseball player, a second baseman, who was selected to play on the All-Star Team. Every Little Leaguer wanted to be an All-Star, because it was the All-Star Team that participated in post-season competition. It was the All-Star Team that was able to compete in the Little League World Series held every year in Williamsport, Pennsylvania. The Little League World Series, with teams from almost the entire civilized world having the opportunity to be World Champions.

In rural America, All-Stars are selected for their abilities, not the position that they played during the regular season. Thus it was that a 10 year old second baseman was moved to the outfield for a game against Berlin, New Jersey. It was about noon on game day when the young All-Star jogged out to his position in left field to catch a few pop ups hit by his coach. The eager young All-Star lost a fly ball in the sun and was hit in the eye. An eye was injured and a dream died that day on a Little League field in Berlin, New Jersey. The ambulance arrived to take the injured left fielder to the hospital and a young boy's life would never be the same. All Joey Fort knew that day as he was rushed to the hospital was that his eye hurt.

After the accident. Joey Fort underwent five operations in three years to try and save the vision in his left eye, and he never played baseball again. The fourth operation to remove a traumatic cataract left him with no lens in his left eye, unable to read, wear glasses or soft contacts. But it was not the pain of the operations that hurt Joey the most, it was the pain of being ostracized by his schoolmates and parents in his community that was worse than the injury. As the hospital bills began to mount, Joey's parents went to the local Little League officials and the All-Star coaches to seek some financial assistance. Unfortunately, what began with a sense of understanding and cooperation, turned into confrontation and a lawsuit was filed by

Joey's parents. The local newspaper took the story and created a fire storm of controversy, because in the 1980s people did not sue Little League Baseball or volunteer coaches. It did not take long for the entire state of New Jersey to be up in arms over the lawsuit, and the case was carried by the wire services all across the United States. The lawsuit filed by the parents on behalf of their son sought $750,000 in damages for the eye injury Joey had incurred. The lawsuit alleged that Joey was never given proper instruction on how to play the outfield, was not shown how to use a glove to shield the sun, and was not given flip-up sun glasses to shield the sun. After several years the case was settled out of court with the two volunteer coaches paying $25,000. Little League Baseball and Pop Warner football ended in Runnemeade, New Jersey after the settlement was announced, because no one in the community wanted to be a volunteer coach and get sued. It was little Joey Fort who got the blame, who was ridiculed, and who was made to feel miserable for what had happened.

After the settlement was announced, panic and fear spread throughout the state of New Jersey because Little League baseball was going to be finished. Politicians joined in the controversy and the New Jersey Legislature passed a bill to protect volunteer coaches from lawsuits. When the bill was being debated before the General Assembly one of the speakers who endorsed the need for the proper training of volunteer coaches and the passage of the bill was Joey Fort's father. New Jersey became the first state in the United States to pass legislation dealing with Youth Sports and volunteer coaches.

Today Joey Fort is Joe Fort who is a 1995 Drexel University graduate with a degree in Mechanical Engineering, married, and gainfully employed. Joe tried soccer after his injury, but eventually joined the high school band and followed his interest in music. If he ever has children, he will not encourage or discourage them from playing youth sport, but if they choose to play, he could see himself volunteering to help coach.

At 10-years-old, Joey Fort became one of the most infamous Little League players in American history, yet he is very proud of his parents for the stand that they took those 17 years ago. Would he wish his experience on anybody else? No, and unfortunately after it was all over the newspapers and other media outlets never wanted to hear the Fort side of the incident.

I tell the story of Joe Fort for two reasons. First we read about lawsuits in newspapers or court documents and all we see are words on a page; we forget that these cases involve real people. It is important to remember that lawsuits are about people, not statistics and that when injuries occur, people suffer.

Second, unfortunately over the last 17 years we have not made a great deal of progress in certifying and training youth sport coaches. Recently a grandfather remarked that when he went to sign his grandson up for soccer, the league officials asked him if he would be able to coach. The grandfather asked what was the criteria for being the soccer coach, and was told that the most important quality was ownership of a van. If a parent had a van and could transport the team to games, that was sufficient to be a coach. A coach of the greatest natural resource America has to offer, our children, and all we want is a drivers license and a van to qualify as coach.

It is the purpose of this book to educate the thousands of people who work with children in a sport setting every day. This book will serve as a resource and guide to help people understand how to provide a better and safer sporting experience. It has been said that the value of law lies not in the happiness it creates, but rather in the misery and suffering it prevents.

Chapter I

The Origin of Youth Sport

Sport is a vital character builder. It molds the youth of our country for their future roles as custodians of the republic . . . Fathers and mothers who would make their sons into men should have them play the game.

Douglas McArthur

The origin of sport goes back to prehistoric times, before the advent of civilization. Richard Swanson and Betty Spears, sports historians, define sport as:

> attitude involving physical prowess and skill, competition, strategy and or chance, and engaged in for the enjoyment and satisfaction of the participant and or others. This definition includes both organized sport and sport for recreational purposes. It includes sport as entertainment and also encompasses professional sport (Swanson and Spears, 1995).

Ancient Olympic Games

Organized sport goes back as far as the ancient Olympic games held every four years at Mount Olympus to honor the Greek gods. Homer wrote about examples of sport in his epic poem the *Iliad*. The Romans with their chariot races and gladiatorial combat took sport to a new level and the Medieval Tournaments kept the sporting tradition alive. Today, in the United States, we talk about grown men playing the games of children and being financially rewarded for their abilities and success. The professional athlete of today is probably not playing a children's game, rather today's children are playing adult games. After all, the ancient Greek Olympic hero or the Roman gladiator or charioteer, the medieval knight, the Native American lacrosse player, the South American Indian ball player and the first American baseball players were all adults, all men who trained for years for their special events. Sport has historically been an adult activity, organized and participated in by adults, for adults, and it has only been in the last century that children have entered the adult world of organized sport. For the ancient participant, sport was a method of practicing or preparing for war, or a means to learn the art of survival. Sport was also the way to achieve fame, honor, prestige and wealth in ancient civilizations. Organized athletic competition has never been for children, it has always been for adults, either as participants or spectators. The Stadium at Mt. Olympus in Greece and the Circus Maximus in Rome are two examples of the value, and popularity placed on sport by two ancient cultures. The college and professional athletes of today are following a tradition that goes back over 3,000 years, it is today's child that is entering unchartered waters.

The Beginnings of Youth Sport in the United States

The founding of Little League Baseball in 1939 is recognized by many as the beginning of the modern Youth Sport movement in the United States. However, adult organized and directed sport for children goes back to the last few decades of the 19th century and the first several decades of the 20th century. It was the Industrial Revolution that helped create the need to establish Youth Sport. The Industrial Revolution altered the American lifestyle forever and created our modern urban society. Thousands of people left the farms and small towns of rural America to migrate to the major industrial centers where they found a new environment and a new culture. Children no longer had fields and farms to run, play and work in, but were confined to apartments and city streets. Farm children were accustomed to having contact with adult parents on a regular basis, but now, living in the city, with parents working in the factories and mills, access was limited. Social problems such as crime, delinquency, child labor, orphans, and unwholesome environments became concerns for residents of big cities. Sarah N. Cleghorn, a social worker in the 1900s wrote: "the golf links be so near the mill that almost every day the laboring children can look out and see the men at play." Children were either working long hours in sweat shops or were running loose on city streets. There was no longer a sense of community; small town America was beginning to disappear. Childhood became recognized as an important stage in human development and muckraker journalists, politicians, citizens and parents became concerned about children. The urban industrialized society was damaging child rearing and weakening the fabric of the American family. Fathers and mothers went off to work and children were left at home with nothing to do, no place to go and little adult supervision. People became interested in trying to manage or occupy the free time of children and sport was seen as a viable option. Organized sport could substitute for rural upbringing, fill the void left by the disappearance of the household economy, provide an early work type experience, and replace the weakened authority of religion (Rader, 1983).

Muscular Christianity

Muscular Christianity, an attempt to use athletes as a means to attract males to Protestant churches, helped begin the Youth Sport movement and later professional "boy workers" added a theory of play derived from Darwin's Theory of Evolution. One inner city youth worker claimed that: "Urban children watch the drunken people, listen to the leader of the gang, hear the shady story, smoke cigarettes and acquire those vicious habits, knowledge and vocabulary which are characteristic of the worst denizens of the city" (Rader, 1983). Combine American migrants with European immigrants and the problems continued to mount for the big cities.

The Values of Team Sport

Our British heritage helped to supply the use of sport as the tonic to cure the ills of society. The British believed that sport could be used to teach good wholesome values. In England the upper class participated in sport to make them better citizens, by learning teamwork, fair play, respect for others, and self discipline. The Duke of Wellington is supposed to have given credit for the victory at Waterloo to the playing fields of Eton. F.D. Boynton, Superintendent of Ithaca Schools wrote in 1904: "What can we offer to the city boy in exchange for paradise lost? His only road to paradise regained is through the gymnasium, the athletic field, and the playground" (Rader, 1983). G. Stanley Hall (President of Clark University in 1900), and Luther Gulick (first President of the Playground Association of America), developed an evolutionary theory of play that could be used to guide men into adulthood. Team sport was a way that adults could encourage the moral and religious growth of young boys. Team sport could develop the highest moral principles, principles of team work, self sacrifice, obedience, self control and loyalty. At the same time that people began advocating the team sport experience as a solution to some inner city problems, educators were struggling with the issue of compulsory attendance in public school. The progressive reform movement helped to increase the school term from four months to nine months and to extend compulsory attendance to age 14. The responsibility for the development of young men then fell to the schools and the sporting experience. What better way to teach young children American values than through the experience of team sport. Respect for rules, teamwork, sportsmanship, success, failure, cooperation, sharing, hard work, could all be learned from a game of baseball.

Public School Athletic League

In 1903 the Public School Athletic League was founded for the express purpose of providing immigrant youths with American culture and values. The responsibility for providing a competitive sporting experience was shared by several organizations. The Public Schools, Public School Athletic League, city playground associations, and national organizations like the YMCA and YWCA all played a role. In addition, several other national youth organizations began at this time, Boys Clubs of America and the Playground Association of America (1906), Boy Scouts and Camp Fire Girls (1910), and the Girl Scouts (1912). Historian Benjamin Rader claimed a manly youth around the turn of the century could be described this way:

> The manly youth cultivated self command and absolute candor; he abhorred display, pretension, sentimentality and capitulation to pain. He insisted on justice and was quick to defend honor with physical prowess; he was physically active, striving to develop the utmost robustness, animal energy and personal courage. His spirit found its truest expression in the out-of-doors, in the refreshing vigor of the countryside and on the athletic field (Rader, 1983).

President Theodore Roosevelt: A Model for Youth Sport

President Theodore Roosevelt once advised the nations boys: "In life, as in a football game, the principle to follow is: hit the line hard, don't foul, and don't shirk, but hit the line hard" (Rader, 1983).

Involvement in sport was seen by many Americans as an essential part of the education of a young man. Competitive sport was a way to replace the basic family values of rural life that had been lost in the big city. The strenuous life of Theodore Roosevelt, was the model for youth sport during the first two decades of the 20th century. However, by the 1920s and early 1930s, educators begin to see some of the abuses of highly organized sport, and concern grew about how much competition was good for preadolescent children (Berryman, 1982). Educators began to pull back from supporting competitive sport for elementary age children as the United States entered the first Golden Age of Sport.

The Golden Age of Sport

In the roaring 20s, sport became extremely popular in America as bigger than life sports heroes made the headlines. Babe Ruth (baseball), Red Grange (football), Bobby Jones (golf) and Bill Tilden (tennis) were just a few examples of athletes that became celebrities. High school, college, and professional sport all became popular, but competitive sport for children fell in disfavor with professional leaders (Coakley, 1978). With sport becoming more and more popular, adults saw the need to step in and organize the sporting experience for children. Practice, scheduled contests, officials, leagues, championships, tournaments, travel, and commercial sponsors were all seen by adults as important for children. There were no curriculum restraints, no ideology, no play theory, the adult-directed youth leagues were shaped by winning. All across the country the present day youth sport model was developing. In 1924 the Cincinnati Community Service started a Baseball tournament for boys under 13 (Berryman, 1982). Tackle football for boys 12 and under began in Denver, Colorado in 1927, and the *Los Angeles Times* conducted a Junior Pentathlon in 1928. In 1929, the year the Stock Market crashed, Pop Warner football was established and the Southern California Tennis Association began a year later in 1930. Milwaukee organized its Stars of Yesterday and Kid Baseball School in 1936, and *Life* magazine did a 1939 feature on a little league football game in Denver. Civic groups, churches, businesses, local merchants, and professional sport all took up the torch of helping to establish youth sport.

Little League Baseball Founded

In 1939, Carl Stotz, a lumber company employee from Williamsport, Pennsylvania founded Little League Baseball. Stotz founded Little League baseball in response to his own frustrations as a youngster with the unsupervised and chaotic play that existed. In Little League baseball there were colorful uniforms, regulation baseballs, outfield fences, dugouts, umpires, and even a player draft system. Adult volunteers would operate Little League baseball just like the professional leagues, but by 1947 there were only 60 teams and about 1,000 players. The United States Rubber Company became a sponsor, the post World War II baby boom began and by 1957 there were almost a million boys on 19,500 teams in 47 states and 22 foreign countries. In 1995, Little League baseball had grown to 196,000

teams, 2.7 million participants in the United States and 3 million participants worldwide (Rader, 1983).

Media Exposure

Little League baseball is to Youth Sport what Xerox is to copies, and
Coca-Cola is to soft drinks, it is still the king. However, three events in
the 1970s altered the picture of Youth Sport. The first is television, and
beginning in the late 60s the broadcasts of tennis and golf created immense
interest in these two individual sports. In tennis Jimmy Connors and
Chris Evert became poster hero's for a whole new generation of young
people. Then the Olympics hit prime time, and sports-like figure skat-
ing, gymnastics, and swimming captured the attention of young and old
alike. Olga Korbut and Mary Lou Retton in gymnastics, and Mark Spitz
in swimming created a new generation of "wannabees" as millions became aware of the fame and financial rewards that could follow Olympic
success. Television, the Olympics, and then soccer, a sport for every
child. Soccer is a sport that adults have never taken to as spectators, but
children have as participants. President Bill Clinton rode to reelection
in 1996 on the strength of the soccer mom vote according to political
analysis. Soccer has become the Youth Sport of the '90s with recreation
leagues, travel, select and elite teams making it possible for children to
play year round.

Participation in Youth Sport

Today, in the United States, it is estimated that at least 25 million young
people from the age of five to 18 are participating in some type of adult directed Youth Sport experience. From A.A.U. basketball, to go-cart racing,
to martial arts, to billiards and table tennis there is some type of organized
Youth Sport for everyone. From community recreation, church and civic
club sponsored, to camps, schools and academies there is an opportunity
for every child to participate. Youth Sport is a part of American culture.
Youth Sport has come a long way in the last century, unfortunately so have
legal problems.

After the Facts

Sports Are Bad for Children

I'm puzzled about American sport. How does it keep escaping the attention of people who worry about the corruption of youth? It's not good enough to say these people have their hands full fighting drugs, pornography and television violence. Sure, those things are terrible for the young, and I wouldn't want my children exposed to them, but neither would I want them exposed to sport as now practiced in the United States.

Consider a few of the traditional high-minded excuses for athletics:

"A sound mind in a sound body"—that was the classic reason for sport. No sensible child who has been subjected to the sports news can hear it nowadays without curling his lips in a sneer.

He has heard too much about the importance of "playing with pain" and multimillion-dollar contracts. It is not "a sound mind in a sound body" that he contemplates when he thinks of sport; it is an avaricious mind in a crippled body.

"Sports build character"—old-timers used to say that. Football coaches were especially fond of it. "Football builds character," they used to say. But show me a child whose parents have mindlessly let him follow football, and I'll show you a child who knows that what football really does is fire coaches who lose.

"It's not whether you win or lose, but how you play the game"— try this one on an American youngster sometime if you want to see a kid roll on the floor with laughter.

Unless he's been sheltered against sports, he knows the great Vince Lombardi's dictum—"Winning is the only thing"—and applauds the latest tennis brat for the swinishness of his winning game.

For the young, the lesson from the field is that rotten manners, greed and determination to win at any cost to body and soul are virtues. Is it really worse having a child hooked on pornography or drugs? Pornography eventually gets boring, a drug habit can be broken, but a child trained to admire toutishness will remain a lout all his life.

For a really bright child, a child who lifts his eyes from the locker room and looks at sport as an institution, the results are even more devastating. Do you want to bring up a child who looks on other people as so much tax-deductible meat?

That's what a kid sees nowadays if you let him read about the owners of professional teams who depreciate their players to cut tax bills.

Do you want to raise your kid to be a finagler? Then let him read the sports pages. He will be exposed to a constant stream of stories about owners extorting sweetheart real-estate and tax deals out of politicians by threatening to move their teams to other cities.

I know, I know—every good American is supposed to become a finagler sooner or later, and you may say, "Why not get the kid thinking that way when he's just a little tot 5 or 6 years old?"

My answer to that is it's a shame that every good American is supposed to become a finagler, and it's time we set better goals, at least for our kids. If we're not willing to start somewhere, we ought to quit whining about the loss of those wonderful old American values that everybody laments.

A good way to start would be to stop children from being exposed to sports, and especially news about the people who own and operate the country's sports system. A child who has been marinated in such stuff in recent years won't even respect his elders, most of whom are probably antiquated enough to think of themselves as fans.

If the kid has half a brain, he can't help realizing that "fan" is just another word for "sap."

How could he not know? He has watched the fans—those dumb jerks—shell out tax money to give the local owner a real-estate break. Then he has heard the fans—those poor dopes—cry about being betrayed when the owner moved his team to the next whistle stop for an even sweeter deal.

If the kid has grown up on sports, he knows a fan is nothing but a dumbbell who's paying taxes to keep the owner in residence until he can locate another town with an even bigger bunch of saps. When this kid sees that his parents are fans, he naturally dreams of growing up to become a chiseler cunning enough to make the old folks carry his share of the tax load.

Imagine the child of higher ambition who yearns to become an educator. What does he dream of after exposure to the sports world? Surely not of running an academy where everyone will be conversant with Ovid and quantum theory. No, he dreams of presiding over a campus operated as a profitable minor-league training camp for professional sports, whose products can be shipped off to the big time before Commencement Day creates the embarrassment of having to give them degrees.

Save the children. Stamp out sports (Baker, 1984).

References

Baker, Russell. "Sports are Bad for Children," *New York Times News Service*, April 29, 1984.

Berryman, Jack W. *Children in Sport*. Human Kinetics, Champaign, Illinois, 1982.

"Child Labor." *Encyclopedia Americana*. 1971.

Coakley, Jay. *Sport in Society*. Mosby, St. Louis, Missouri, 1978.

Lumpkin, Angela. *Physical Education and Sport*. Times/Mirror/Mosby College Publishing, St. Louis, Missouri, 1990.

Michener, James. *Sports in America*. Random House, New York, New York, 1976.

Mihoces, Gary. "Lawsuits Overshadow Youth League Playoffs," *USA Today*, August 17, 1995.

Rader, Benjamin G. *American Sports*. Third Edition. Prentice-Hall, Englewood Cliffs, New Jersey, 1983.

Swanson, Richard A. and Betty Spears. *History of Sport and Physical Education in the United States*. Fourth Edition. Brown and Benchmark, Dubuque, Iowa, 1995.

Chapter 2

Litigation and Youth Sport

Lawsuits are a search for the truth.

Joseph DeLucia

No one wants a sport participant to be injured. In sport activities, however, there is always the possibility of injury no matter how carefully proper procedures are observed. In like manner, no one wants to be a defendant in a lawsuit. Today there is unusual interest in youth sport and the unprecedented participation in youth sport is accompanied by a record number of sport-related lawsuits. The fact that an injury occurs does not necessarily mean that the coach is negligent or liable for damages. There are no definitive criteria for determining what is negligent behavior since each case stands on its own merit. The threat of expensive litigation, however, is very real and ever-present in today's litigious world. It is helpful and necessary for all associated with youth sport to understand the legal aspects of the activities so that guidelines can be established that will provide safety for the participant and protection for those who administer and coach in the youth sport program.

Lawsuits

Americans have a love-hate relationship with lawsuits. Author Peter Carlson claims that lawsuits are the middle class equivalent of the drive-by shooting, the modern answer to the duel, the more civilized alternative to the hit man. The lawsuit is the twentieth century version of meet me out back and we will settle this man to man, only now it is my lawyer can whip your lawyer (Carlson, 1992). Consumer advocate, and lawyer, Ralph Nader, calls lawsuits the "mark of civilization." Whether you agree or disagree with the number of lawsuits, the fact remains that in 1989 there were almost 18 million new civil suits filed in American Courts, or one for every ten Americans (Carlson, 1992).

Extreme Lawsuits

Some of the lawsuits are extreme at times. For example, a South Texas man borrowed his neighbors lawn mower and while mowing his own yard, slipped and pulled the mower over his own foot. The injured man sued his neighbor for $235,00. An unsympathetic Lone Star jury, however, refused to award the man anything (Landers, 1995). In New York City. a teacher slipped on a puddle of milk while teaching soccer on the school playground and suffered a ruptured quadricep. The teacher sued the New York City Board of Education and a jury awarded the plaintiff $908,000 in damages (Appenzeller and Baron, 1995). A woman sued a man for $5,000 because he swore at her in traffic and on the trial court level she won $2,500. The decision was reversed on appeal because she failed to demonstrate that her distress was above what a reasonable person could endure (Landers, 1995). A Fort Worth Texas man filed a lawsuit against Elvis Presley Enterprises claiming that the King of Rock and Roll faked his own death to run off and live a normal life. Probably every American has heard about Stella Liebeck, the 81 year old woman, who spilled hot coffee in her lap after leaving a McDonalds drive through in Albuquerque, New Mexico (Verchick, 1997). Liebeck sued the hamburger chain and was awarded $2.9 million, $200,000 compensatory damages, and $2.7 million in punitive damages.

Yes, Americans have a love-hate relationship with lawsuits, we hate them, believe they are frivolous and excessive unless we are the injured party, and then it is a different story.

Good or bad, lawsuits are an important part of the our culture. In the early 1760s, the Reverend Charles Woodmason, an Anglican Preacher, noticed a passion for lawsuits in South Carolina. Woodmason wrote: "This passion for lawsuits and prosecutions does not arise so much from a love of justice, but from a corruption of the human heart.... On the least umbrage, pique, or misunderstanding, they will warrant their neighbor." (Carlson, 1992) In the early 1800s French historian Alex de Tocqueville observed that Americans have an extraordinary tendency to look to the courts to resolve their disputes (Lubell, 1987). Even old honest Abe Lincoln, a fair country lawyer in his day, gave this advice about lawsuits in 1850: "Discourage litigation. Persuade your neighbors to compromise whenever you can. Point out to them how the nominal winner is often a real loser — in fees, expenses, and waste of time"(Landers, 1995). We have not taken Lincoln's advice to heart, in fact, the number of lawsuits continues to sky-rocket, and we have become the most litigious society on the planet. Former United States Vice President Dan Quayle, a lawyer, in a speech addressing the American Bar Association claimed that the litigation explosion was bleeding the American economy of $80 billion in direct costs and as much as $300 billion in indirect cost each year.

Reasons for Increased Litigation

Lawsuits and litigation are part of the American tradition of jurisprudence, part of our culture and that reality is beginning to be felt on the Youth Sport level. In my opinion there are ten reasons for the litigation explosion and why Youth Sport is being caught up in the explosion.

Number 1

In the United States there is a right to sue. We can sue anybody at any time for any reason and it happens frequently. The old common sense approach to the law as practiced by Andy Taylor, as Justice of the Peace in Mayberry, has given way to popular television shows like *L.A. Law*, *The People's Court*, *Divorce Court*, and *Judge Judy*. Americans have watched enough television to see that litigation can be a solution to a problem. Television has made Americans more aware of our legal system.

Number 2

There is a myth currently popular in the United States that people can participate in vigorous physical sport and recreational activities without fear of accident or injury. We have "fat free," "sugar free" food, and now "risk free" sport. The very nature of sport means that there is movement, contact, and sometimes even collisions which create risk. Whether it is cliff diving, hang gliding, or a pick-up basketball game, sport involves risk. Risk is part of the excitement. However, many Americans today do not want to accept responsibility for injuries, we want to blame someone or something. To be able to participate in dangerous activities, but never suffer any pain or hardship is not realistic, but it is the American ideal today.

Number 3

Injuries are expensive. When an injury does occur in sport, with the high cost of medical treatment, there is usually an insurance shortfall. Most insurance companies will not pay 100% of a claim which means there will be some out of pocket expense for the family of the victim, regardless of fault or blame. People see a lawsuit as a way to help cover the expense of medical treatment and to right a wrong, real or imagined.

Number 4

Currently in the United States we also have the doctrine of entitlement, when people are hurt, they need to be taken care of. We have a nation of victims and we feel sorry for people when they are injured. Jurors see accident victims as being entitled to financial relief. Jurors tend to be sympathetic to the injured party and want to soften their burden in a humanistic manner. According to Carlson: "the culture of litigation has skewed the American psyche, tilting it away from taking responsibility for ones misfortunes or cursing the fates and toward blaming it all on somebody else, preferably somebody with deep pockets or good insurance coverage (Carlson, 1992). Victims believe that some form of redress is needed. Somebody is going to pay, and it should be the party that caused the injury. Jurors see insurance companies as a painless way to offer relief to a victim, because insurance companies have money and the victim needs help (Lubell, 1987).

Number 5

Insurance companies do not enjoy paying out large jury awards to victims, and insurance companies view lawsuits as a bottom line issue. What is the least expensive route to take when looking at litigation. There are three options, go to court and win, go to court and lose, and settle the case before it goes to court. The facts of the case do not matter, what is the cost and what is the cheapest way out of a bad situation. To settle a case out of court is usually the least expensive alternative.

Number 6

Insurance companies have a tendency to settle lawsuits out of court. It has been estimated that 90% of American lawsuits never come to trial (Carlson, 1992). Organizations involved in lawsuits do not want all the negative publicity that comes with a trial, so there is pressure to settle and avoid public scrutiny. Insurance companies do not want to spend money on lawyer fees and then take a chance on a sympathetic jury that might award an excessive sum in damages.

Number 7

Lawyers today understand the economics of litigation and they realize that 90% of lawsuits will be settled. This rush to settle has been given as one of the reasons for the frivolous lawsuits that we read about. For a personal injury lawyer, a settled lawsuit is a good pay day, with very little time and expense. There is now an organization called, "The Citizens Against Lawsuit Abuse," which is trying to publicize frivolous lawsuits. Recently it has been suggested, regarding tort reform, that the United States adopt the British model of litigation, where the loser in the lawsuits pays the court costs. However, there has been no rush to punish lawyers who bring the frivolous cases to court.

Number 8

It has been suggested by some that one of the reasons for the increased number of lawsuits today is that we have too many lawyers. Currently over 70% of all lawyers in the world practice in the United States. We have one lawyer for every 310 Americans. Lawyers today advertise on television, radio, billboards, have toll free numbers and will work for free, it is called a contingency basis. Lawyers market their skills to people who have been injured, people who need a friend, an advocate. Do we have too many lawyers in the United States, and are lawyers in order to survive creating an atmosphere of fear:

> The culture of litigation produces the fear of litigation, which causes people to hire lawyers for defensive purposes, which causes a greater demand for lawyers, which produces more lawyers, who produce more lawsuits, which cause more fear of lawsuits, which causes a greater demand for lawyers, which produces more lawyers, who produce move, etc. (Carlson, 1992).

Even William Shakespeare suggested years ago that the just thing to do is "kill all the lawyers."

Number 9

Insurance companies blame lawyers and the lawyers blame the insurance companies, but the media has also played a significant role in the increase in lawsuits. When people read and hear about huge damage awards and settlements like the McDonald's' case, it has an influence on the average person. Publicity about lawsuits creates interest and interest creates new lawsuits. In law enforcement, police talk about copy-cat crimes, well how many lawsuits are created because of what an individual saw or read. How many Americans see a big lawsuit as the equivalent of hitting the lottery. Unlike the lottery where participants choose to participate, in a lawsuit everybody pays one way or another. There is no free lunch in civil litigation, we all pay in the long run.

Number 10

Youth Sport today in the United States is big business and an important part of our culture. We have turned games for children into a national passion and have elevated sport to a level of importance beyond all reality. The Youth Sport athlete of today is not just a nine or eleven-year-old boy or girl. The young athlete of today is the Olympic or professional star of tomorrow. That Little Leaguer is going to earn millions, going to be the next Michael Jordan or Tiger Woods. There will be Nike and Reebok endorsements, and at the very least a four-year college scholarship. Stardom in sports is big money and when the future hero is injured or not allowed to play, there is a major financial loss. Pro athletes are no longer men and women playing a child's game, they are Odysseus and Achilles, they are multi-million dollar corporations. We no longer have children playing children's games, we have children playing adult games for fame and fortune.

In the old days the volunteer coach, official or administrator would hear the word thanks, but today they may be more likely to hear the words, "I'll sue." Regardless of the reasons, we are seeing more and more lawsuits in Youth Sport and that trend will continue into the next century. The Youth Sport administrator, coach, and official need to be aware of what the legal responsibilities are in this litigious society. It is critical for people in Youth Sport to understand the legal system and its ramifications.

Tort Law

Purpose of Law

The restraint that accompanies every athlete onto the playing field is the law. The definition of the law according to Mr. Webster is "the principles and regulations established by a government or other authority and applicable to people, whether by legislation or by custom enforced by judicial decision" (Random House, 1991). The purpose of the law is to allow individuals to live together in a society, to protect and at the same time provide an element of freedom for those individuals. The law is the rules of the game that a society has established, what is right and what is wrong. Imagine trying to drive through any major city today at rush hour without benefit of any stop lights, speed limits, or policemen. What would normally be an adventure, would suddenly become a disaster. It is the purpose of the law to bring order out of chaos, to allow people the opportunity to live together in a peaceful society.

Sources of Law

The first step in understanding American law is to know that there are two sources of law. There is statutory law which is law made by the legislative branch of the government and there is common or case law which consists of actual judicial decisions.

Bodies of Law

In the United States we have two different bodies of laws, criminal law and civil law. Criminal law is the type of law that most Americans are familiar with from watching police shows on television. Criminal law seeks to protect people by establishing a series of rules and regulations about what can not be done. It is against criminal law to murder, rape, rob, or commit arson. Criminal law is derived from statutory law and is produced by elected representatives of the people. When someone breaks a criminal law there is an established punishment for the offender. We do not hang people anymore for stealing horses, or cut off a hand for shoplifting, but we still execute people for the most serious crimes. Law enforcement agencies from the local police and sheriff to the state trooper and F.B.I. have the responsibility of enforcing the rules and regulations and bringing offenders to justice. A person arrested and accused of a crime has the right to a trial and may be found innocent or guilty. In criminal proceedings it is the state that brings the charges and it is society that has been violated.

The majority of Youth Sport cases at this time fall under the body of civil law. Civil law is designed to help settle disputes between individuals, especially when some one believes they too have been wronged. Civil law developed from the English tradition of common law or case law. In common law tradition, decisions in court cases, established precedents, or guidelines for later cases and other judges to follow. In order for there to be consistency in civil law, judges must rely on past judicial decisions when making new decisions. Using past decisions is referred to as the doctrine of *stare decisis*, a term derived from the legal maxim, to stand by the decision (Dougherty, 1994). The purpose of civil law then is to settle disputes between individuals, groups or businesses, instead of resorting to violence or bloodshed. When a person has been injured, that person can go to civil court for relief. A civil action is a lawsuit brought by one or more individuals, against another individual, group, business or the government. Civil law seeks to settle the dispute and to recover damages to make the injured party whole again (Wong, 1994). The injured party is made whole again through the recovery of damages, usually monetary awards, made by the party that inflicted the injury or committed the wrong. Civil law involves injuries caused by an action that in and of itself is not a criminal act. No statutory or criminal law has been broken but someone believes himself/herself to be injured or wronged and the courts have to be the referee. It is the responsibility of the injured party (the plaintiff) to initiate the legal action against the other party (the defendant). The plaintiff will bring a lawsuit against the defendant to civil court and ask to recover damages for the injury suffered. In civil court there is no guilt ir innocence, either the defendant is responsible for the injury or not.

Tort: A Legal Wrong

When there has been a wrong or injury suffered by one party as the result of what somebody else has done, we refer to the cause of action as a tort. Tort is a French term meaning a wrong, injury, the opposite of right (Black, 1951). A tort is a legal wrong committed upon the person or property independent of a contract. A tort may be either:

1. A direct invasion of some legal right of the individual.
2. The infraction of some public duty by which special damage occurred to the individual.
3. A violation of some private obligation by which like damage occurs to the individual (Black, 1951).

The injury can be direct or indirect to the person, property, or reputation. Torts may be either intentional or unintentional and are usually divided into three classes:

1. Intentional tort: intent to commit the act and intent to harm the plaintiff.
2. Reckless misconduct or gross negligence: intent to commit the act, but no intent to harm the plaintiff.
3. Unintentional tort or negligence: no intent to commit the act and no intent to harm the plaintiff, but a failure to exercise reasonable care (Wong, 1994).

Personal Injury

A personal injury whether administered intentionally, wantonly, or negligently constitutes a tort and a general rule is that a person injured by the commission of a tort is entitled to the actual monetary compensation for the injury sustained. The legal question of responsibility for an injury is addressed by tort liability, which is measured by the scope of the duty owed by the defendant. The duty of tort law is to avoid causing harm to others and that duty may be to an individual, member of a class, group, or team. Just because someone is injured in sports does not automatically create a tort or a lawsuit. Injuries and accidents still happen where there is no fault or blame. Justice J. Neal in *Swanson v. Wabash College* (1987) observed that:

> Injuries in sports are not only predictable but a certainty . . . all baseball players have been hit by balls or bats, injured while sliding or colliding on a base path, at a base or with other fielders while fielding the ball . . . By the very nature of play, no coach or manager can possibly prevent such occurrences. All persons who play ball know this and assume the risks.

Responsibility for the Injury: Negligence

Determining the responsibility for an injury is where the concept of negligence comes into the picture. Negligence is the failure to exercise that degree of care which under the circumstances, the law requires for the protection of others (Stern, 1981). A common definition of negligence, is the failure to exercise the same degree of care as a hypothetical reasonable and prudent person would exercise in the same situation (Phay, 1977). Negligence is conduct that can be active or passive, conduct that falls below the standards established by the courts to protect other individuals from harm. Negligence is what juries and judges say it is based on case law. Negligence can be an act of commission, like allowing children to play tag with bows and arrows, or it can be passive, such as not providing proper emergency response or forgetting to have water available during hot summer practices. The doctrine of negligence rests on the duty of every person to exercise care in his conduct toward other people (Black, 1951). Negligence may just be the embodiment of the Golden Rule into case law, do unto others as you would have them do unto you. The law of negligence is not found in any written codes, and unfortunately it sometimes takes years of testimony and expert witnesses to determine what a reasonable and prudent person would do in the same situation. Negligence can be doing something the wrong way, or not doing the right thing at the right time. The key to understanding the concept of negligence is, did the action or lack of action place someone in danger, and cause an injury? Reasonable, prudent, the law of negligence is based on reasonable care and conduct under any and all circumstances. "In fact no court has held a defendant liable where there was substantial evidence that the defendant acted with prudence and caution in the performance of his duties" (Appenzeller, 1983).

Elements of a Lawsuit

In a lawsuit to recover damages for an injury, the plaintiff must prove four elements to be present for the action or inaction to be considered negligent. There has to be:

1. A duty of care owed, a duty is an obligation requiring the action to conform to a certain standard of conduct for the protection of others.
2. Breach of duty is a failure to conform or provide the standard of care required.
3. Actual and proximate cause, there has to be a relationship between the injury and what the defendant did or did not do.
4. Damages, there has to be actual loss, an actual injury. Just because some one could have been hurt is not sufficient to prove negligence (Appenzeller, 1983).

Defense Against Negligence

When there has been an injury in Youth Sport and the claim of negligence has been brought against the defendant in a civil suit, there have traditionally been several defenses which defendants have used. The following are the most common defenses employed by defendants in a tort action involving the charge of negligence:

1. Lack of negligence
2. Contributory negligence
3. Comparative negligence
4. Assumption of risk
5. Charitable immunity, Statute of Limitations and Good Samaritan Status (Wong, 1994).
6. Act of God.

The best defense against a charge of negligence is to show that there was no negligence. The defendant can demonstrate that one of the four elements required for negligence was not present in the particular case. The defendant may also show that he or she did exercise reasonable care in fulfilling their duty or obligation to the injured party.

Contributory Negligence

In the defense of contributory negligence the defendant demonstrates that what the plaintiff did or did not do caused the injury. If the plaintiff did not behave as a reasonable and prudent person then under the principle of contributory negligence the plaintiff can not recover damages. "Contributory negligence prevents a person from receiving damages if he or she is at fault to even the slightest degree in causing his own injury" (Appenzeller, 1983).

Comparative Negligence

Comparative negligence is the tort law equivalent of it takes two to tango. There has been an injury, both sides should take some responsibility and it will be up to the court to prorate the damages in some states. There is a dollar amount placed on the injury, and as long as the plaintiff is less than 50% responsible, then the plaintiff will recover damages based on the percentage of responsibility. In most states, when the plaintiff is more responsible for causing the injury, then no damages will be awarded.

Assumption of Risk

Assumption of risk means that the plaintiff understood that the activity engaged in was dangerous. Assumption of risk is like the motto *caveat emptor*, or "buyer beware," the person knows that hang gliding, rock climbing, or sky diving involves risk and the chance of injury. Since we are a society that does not always want to take responsibility for our own actions, this defense has been challenged frequently as of late. There are several limitations to the assumption of risk doctrine:

1. If by reason of age or lack of information, experience, intelligence, or judgment, the plaintiff does not understand the risk involved in a situation he will not be taken to assume the risk.
2. A plaintiff does not assume a risk of harm unless he voluntarily accepts the risk.
3. The plaintiff's acceptance of a risk is not voluntary if the defendant's tortious conduct has left him no reasonable alternative cause of conduct in order to . . . exercise or protect a right or privledge of which the defendant has no right to deprive him (Appenzeller, 1983).

Assumption of risk is not a very popular defense at this time in civil lawsuits.

Charitable Immunity

Years ago churches, YMCAs and other charitable organizations were immune from litigation, because they were charities, they were there to help. In the case of *Benton v. YMCA of Westfield* the court was very critical of the doctrine of charitable immunity (Benton, 1957) when it said:

> A charity should not be permitted to inflict injury upon some individual without a right of redress, merely in order to bestow charity upon others, because the result would be to compel the victim to contribute to the charity against his will.

The Superior Court of New Jersey added:

> The emphasis of the law generally has been a liability for wrong doing, rather than immunity. The maxim is that all men stand equal before the law, all should be bound alike or excused alike.

The Doctrine of Charitable Immunity is not a very good defense to use in the 1990s and many states have modified the doctrine.

Statute of Limitations and Good Samaritan Statutes

Many states today have Statute of Limitation and Good Samaritan Statutes. Statute of limitations are mandatory deadlines that plaintiffs have for filing a lawsuit. If the time expires, the courts will not accept the case, no matter what. Good Samaritan Statutes have traditionally been laws to protect people who attempted to help another person in need. The Good Samaritan Statutes do not protect anyone who has any type of relationship or duty to the injured party. Historically these statutes were used to protect doctors and nurses who stopped to help an accident victim. Someone who stops to help and then makes the situation worse or causes additional injury would have a difficult time using the Good Samaritan Statute successfully.

Protective Legislation for Volunteer Coaches

Several states, because of lawsuits involving Volunteer Youth Sport Coaches, have attempted to pass legislation to protect coaches from lawsuits. So far the legislative efforts have not been successful.

The best defense is to do what a reasonable person would do in that same situation and that is why we study legal cases, to learn what is prudent and reasonable. We study history to learn from the past and to try and avoid previous mistakes. A court case is a history, a history of what happened and why we are in court. We study common law to learn what worked and what did not in a certain situation. Just as military commanders study past battles, we study past litigation so as not to repeat the mistakes of our predecessors.

How a Case Is Presented in Court

The Complaint

In reality the procedure is as follows: the injured person who is known as the plaintiff institutes a law suit by filing a complaint in which he summarizes his contentions as to why he is entitled to recover damages. A copy of the complaint must be delivered to the party against whom the law suit is directed (defendants).

The Answer

The defendants file an answer to the complaint in which they set forth their various defenses which generally include a denial that they are at fault in causing the injury. It may include such affirmative defenses as contributory negligence or governmental immunity. In appropriate cases the defendants originally sued may join other parties whom they claim to be at fault for the purpose of recovering contribution or full indemnity.

The Trial

After a waiting period which varies in time, depending on the complexity of the case and the relative congestion of the court docket, the case will come to trial. The case will ordinarily be tried before a judge and jury in what is referred to as the lower court. It is the function of the judge to preside over the trial to rule on the admissibility of evidence, to decide whether the plaintiff has offered sufficient evidence to entitle him to recover damages, and to instruct the jury as to the law of the case which the jury would need to understand in order to arrive at a verdict. (At the close of presentation of all the evidence the judge has the right to dismiss the case if it appears there is insufficient evidence to warrant a recovery.)

The judge also has a right to set the verdict of the jury aside if he is convinced that a miscarriage of justice has occurred. In this case it would be necessary for the case to be retried before another jury.

Jury's Function

In some cases the parties elect to waive a jury trial and the judge sits as both judge and jury. The jury's function is to determine the true facts based upon the evidence presented to them and upon the law of the case as given to them by the judge. This would include a decision as to whether the defendants were at fault, whether the plaintiff was also at fault, and the amount of damages the plaintiff should recover.

Right to Appeal

The parties would have the right to appeal to a higher court if dissatisfied with the results of the trial. The higher court, which is known as an appellate court, would not retry the case but would review the record of the trial in order to determine whether prejudicial error had been committed during the trial which prevented the appealing party form obtaining a fair trial.

Among the items which would be reviewed upon appeal are rulings of the trial judge as to exclusion or admission of evidence and his charge to the jury as to the law of the case. If the higher court should find prejudicial error the case would be remanded (sent back) to the trial court for a new trial before another jury.

A Legal Prizefight

Imagine a lawsuit as a Heavyweight Championship Boxing match. The challenger is the plaintiff, he wants justice, an attempt to beat the champion. The Heavyweight Champion is the defendant, he has the belt, and does not want to be bothered by another challenger. The Challenger (Plaintiff) throws down the gauntlet, and begins the prefight preparation by hiring an agent or lawyer to negotiate with the champion (defendant). The challenger (plaintiff) begins the proceedings by filing a complaint against the champion (defendant). The challenger (plaintiff) accuses the champion (defendant) of causing an injury and the challenger (plaintiff) wants satisfaction in the ring (lower court). A copy of the complaint is delivered to the champion (defendant) so that he knows who has been injured and what the injury is. The champion hires an agent (lawyer) to answer the complaint and explain why the challenger (plaintiff) should not be awarded damages or the Heavyweight Title.

After the initial complaint and answer have been established, the two managers (lawyers) explore various options during the prefight discovery period. The two managers (lawyers) do not really want to see their boxers actually have to fight it out in the ring (court) because someone might actually get hurt. While the managers (lawyers) are negotiating for the seize of the purse, cable, and HBO rights the two contestants have to go into training to prepare for the bout. Both sides establish separate training centers (camps) and hire expert coaches (witnesses) to help get ready for the battle.

The Title Bout finally has a location, but it is not Vegas or Atlantic City but in a lower court. The ring (courtroom) is made ready, the supporters of both contestants come to watch and a referee (Trial Judge) is selected to make sure that both sides play fair. The referee (Trial Judge) is neutral and wants to make sure that there are no low blows or rabbit punches thrown. A panel of judges (jury) is selected to observe the fight and to decide who wins. The judges (jury) have to listen to the referee (Trial Judge) in case he penalizes one side or the other. It is the referee (Trial Judge) who enforces the rules of the ring (lower court). If one of the contestants can not maintain a good defense the referee (Trial Judge) may end the fight before it ever gets started (summary judgment). Once the fight begins it is up to the judges (jury) to keep score and record the jabs and knockdowns. The biggest difference in the ring (trial court) and in the actual Heavyweight Bout, is that it is the two managers (lawyers) that exchange the jabs, and punches, instead of the two boxers. The challenger (plaintiff) and champion (defendant) get to sit over in the corner and watch the two managers (lawyers) fight it out.

Function of Judges

The judges (trial jury) function is to watch and listen to the two managers (lawyers) and the expert coaches (witnesses), follow the instructions of the referee (trial judge) and make a decision on who wins and who loses. The judges (jury) keep their scores secret, so nobody knows who has won or lost until they tell the referee (Trial Judge). Sometimes the champion (defendant) and the challenger (plaintiff) will not want a panel of judges (jury) to decide the issue, but will let the referee (Trial Judge) be both referee and jury.

If the champion (defendant) wins, then he keeps the Heavyweight Title Belt and he has to pay his manager (lawyer) and expert coach (witnesses) for jobs well done. If the challenger (plaintiff) wins the bout, then the decision has to be made as to how much the new champion should be compensated. Traditionally the new champion is paid by the former champion (defendant) for the injury that the old champion (defendant) had caused. The challenger (plaintiff) wants to be made whole for the physical, emotional, or psychological suffering that the old champion (defendant) inflicted.

Right to a Rematch

Both parties have the right to ask for a rematch (appeal) if either party is dissatisfied with the results of the bout. The rematch would be held at a new site, or ring (Appellate Court), but the contestants would not actually fight again. A new referee (Appellate Judge) would be brought in to review the facts of the first fight. The new referee (Appellate Judge) would review the rulings and decision of the first referee to determine if the first bout (trial) was a fair fight. If the new referee (Appellate Judge) finds that there was an error in the first bout (trial) he can reverse the first decision. The new referee (Appellate Judge) can also send both combatants back into the fight again with a new referee (Judge) and new judges (jury). The new referee (Appellate Judge) can also approve the results of the first bout and let the decision stand.

Right to Appeal

If either contestant is unhappy with the decision of the second referee (Appellate Judge), the contestants can go before the Boxing Commissioner (Supreme Court). The Boxing Commissioner (Supreme Court) may choose to let the early decision stand or the Commissioner (Supreme Court) may reverse the decision of the two lower referees (Appellate Court and Trial Court). The Boxing Commissioner (Supreme Court) does not allow the two contestants to box again, rather the commissioner reviews the tapes of the earlier bout for errors in proceedings or rulings. The Boxing Commissioner (Supreme Court) will not even see or listen to the two opponents but will listen to only arguments from the two managers (lawyers). Once the Boxing Commissioner (Supreme Court) rules that decision is final. The Defending Champion or the challenger wins, and if the challenger wins, he will be awarded a monetary prize for the victory.

Defendants and Plaintiffs, lawyers and lawsuits, litigation has become very much like a heavyweight championship fight. Damages may be awarded in the millions to plaintiffs, and defendants see their life and career flash before them in a courtroom. The trend to settle disputes in a court room will continue, and it is important for individuals working in Youth Sport to understand the legal process.

What to Do if Involved in a Lawsuit

The question must arise, "What do I do when something happens that may lead to a lawsuit?"

The answer is simple — call your insurance carrier and your lawyer, in that order. This will permit a prompt investigation of the entire case when all events are still fresh in everyone's mind, so that the actual facts may be accurately preserved for presentation later, perhaps year later. It will also protect you against taking any action that could prejudice your position at a later date (Appenzeller and Appenzeller, 1980).

Be sure to keep detailed notes on everything that you know or can remember about what happened, including names and addresses of all potential witnesses, even those people who say they don't know anything. Many times, under skillful questioning, they know much more than they think.

Be reluctant to discuss any aspect of the case without the advice of your attorney, particularly to the news media. This should not imply that you are trying to "cover up" or "hide" anything, but merely that any public statement should be delayed until all the facts are known. Many times statements are made at or about the time of an incident which later turn out not to be the true facts at all after an investigation has been completed.

Trials resulting form lawsuits are actually relatively simple mechanisms to understand, but are difficult and expensive to use. Your chances of being involved in litigation are greatly reduced if you conduct your activities as carefully as possible, use safe, well-maintained equipment and disclose as much as possible to participants and parents (Appenzeller and Appenzeller, 1980).

Many people do not realize that anyone can file a lawsuit against anybody for just about anything, but before a recovery can be obtained liability must be proven. Before liability can be established in a typical case, a breach of duty or violation of a right must be proved by the allegedly aggrieved party. This proof comes in almost all cases at the trial of the lawsuit, anywhere from six months to five years after the lawsuit is stated. Fortunately, in some respects, many legitimate lawsuits are settled before trial or even before a lawsuit is filed (Appenzeller and Appenzeller, 1980).

Franklin Roosevelt once stated that the only thing we have to fear is fear itself, and we do not want people to constantly be afraid of being sued. The best way to overcome fear is through knowledge, through education. This book is about educating the thousands and thousands of adults who work and give of their time to provide sport for millions of children and young adults. The Roman Quintilian once said that, "Education is not what you are able to remember, but the things you can not forget." May the information in this book provide answers and guidelines to adults so that Youth Sport will be safer, and better for our nation's children.

After the Facts

Players Pay for Parents' Values Debate

Ten-year-old Matthew Bartl, a catcher on the Lillian Barracudas baseball team, knew there would be trouble the day he unwrapped his new uniform last month.

Emblazoned on the front of the team jersey was the name of the team's sponsor, C and J Video, owned by the father of Barracuda outfielder David Bryan.

The Bartl family, and most other members of the Elberta Christian and Missionary Alliance Church, don't patronize Bryan's store because among its 3,000 movies are about 500 X-rated films.

Wearing the C and J logo would be "advertising bad videos and selling pornography," Matthew said. So Matthew, whose father is the team manager, and three of his teammates showed up for their first game in T-shirts minus the sponsor's name.

That has splintered this small, rural community on the Gulf of Mexico like a broken wooden bat, pitting neighbors against each other as the national culture wars played out in pint-size form. It has provoked game boycotts by the players, a lawsuit and finally the disbanding of the Barracudas with the intervention of a judge.

"They have punished all the children," said Jennifer Nicholas, a Lillian native who had no objection to her son, Wade, 9, wearing the sponsor's name on his uniform.

When Matthew and his teammates refused to wear the official jersey, some of the other parents, led by video store owner David Bryan and team assistant Darren Miller, whose wife, Stephanie, manages the video store, cited a rule requiring Dixie Youth League uniforms to be, well, uniform. They demanded that all the children dress in the official jersey.

Calvin Bartl, Matthews father, who is a minister at Elberta, contacted the American Center for Law and Justice, an advocacy group founded by televangelist Pat Robertson.

Bryan "has the right to sell and advertise his videos," Bartl said, "but we also have a right not to advertise for him." The boys, who are assigned randomly to teams, didn't know who their sponsor was until the uniforms arrived.

Lillian's locale and natural beauty—it abuts both the Gulf of Mexico and Perdidi Bay—made it ripe for a culture clash.

While the landscape remains dominated by grazing cattle and tractors, in recent years the cows have had to share the land with horses and houses, as suburbanites surged across a new bridge that links rural Baldwin County, Ala., with bustling Pensacola, Fla.

Conservative churches such as the Christian and Missionary Alliance, where Calvin Bartl preaches, remain the focus for many in Lillian.

But there are other social offerings, from taverns to Bryan's video store. Bryan seeks to straddle both worlds. He put up $400 for uniforms and bats and balls for the Barracudas and advertises in a shoppers' newspaper to the tourists and military personnel in Pensacola, where an Escambia County ordinance prohibits the sale or rental of adult movies.

The only indication that the store rents sexually explicit tapes is a large sign out front that promises "all kinds of movies" inside.

Store manager Miller said the X-rated movies are stored in a windowless trailer attached to the store, and can be reached only by request.

The ACLJ assigned the case to its Alabama legal director, Stuart Roth, who also is defending an Alabama judge fighting for the right to display a copy of the Ten Commandments in his courtroom.

On May 1, Roth filed a lawsuit in Baldwin County Circuit Court, charging that the requirement that the video advertisement show on the shirts was a violation of the religious convictions of the four boys.

"It is unfortunate that we have come to the point in this nation where 10-year-old boys must, as a prerequisite for playing ... baseball, act as human billboards for a business that rents and sells adult videos," Roth said.

Roth cited Dixie Youth Baseball's code of ethics, which says it is the league's intent to "promote and help build a program that will result in obedient, patriotic and God-fearing youngsters."

To accomplish that, the league code says, "teams shall be sponsored only by organizations whose activities or products are not detrimental to the welfare of youth."

Were those rules strictly enforced, said Jennifer Nicholas, "there won't be anybody other than farmers who can sponsor a team." She noted that other sponsors include a restaurant that serves alcohol and a community club "that's nothing more than a bar and gambling hall."

Judge Lyn Stuart granted Roth a temporary restraining order on May 1 that allowed the four boys to play two additional games in their generic uniforms, helping the Barracudas start their season with three victories.

But when the no-name quartet showed up for the fourth game, the Dixie Youth League umpire refused to let them take the field, citing the uniform rule.

With Matthew Bartl and the three others stuck on the bench, the Barracudas lost, 4–3, to Elberta.

That apparently was the last game the Barracudas will play this year. The team disbanded last Wednesday after the quarreling parents were unable to reach an out-of-court compromise, even after Bryan bought new shirts that carried only his name, and no mention of his business.

But for Bartl and the three other families, not standing up for their religious beliefs "would be immoral," the preacher said.

Some of the other parents think Bartl has been too eager to mix religion and baseball in the past. Last year, they said, he had to be asked not to send out team notices on church stationery, and not to "witness" to the boys on the team.

Store manager Miller accused Bartl and other protesters of "grandstanding on the shoulders of these boys."

If they were looking for an issue, she said, they should have protested in previous years, when Bryan sponsored teams in other leagues.

The dispute, and the attention it attracted in Alabama, has disgusted many people, including Stuart, who finally told the warring parents that the team should be disbanded. So the Lillian Barracudas are no more.

At least for this season.

While their parents argue and sue, the boys remain friends.

Until they can play together again in their league, they are making plans to play pickup games against the peewee boys team and an older girls' softball team.

"We should have worn different T-shirts instead of getting split up. We all wanted to be on the same team," said Matthew Bartl, a fourth-grader.

Barracuda outfielder Cody Miller, who is "fixing to turn 9" on Monday, said of the dispute, "I don't like it and I hope it stops" (Baker, 1996).

References

American Jurisprudence. Jurisprudence Publishers, Inc., Rochester, New York, 1974.

Appenzeller, Herb. *From the Gym to the Jury*. The Michie Company, Charlottesville, Virginia, 1970.

Appenzeller, Herb. *The Right to Participate*. The Michie Company, Charlottesville, Virginia, 1983.

Appenzeller, Herb and Ron Baron. "Puddle of Milk Leads to $908,000 Verdict," *From the Gym to the Jury*, Greensboro, North Carolina, vol. 7, no. 5, p. 1, 1995.

Appenzeller, Herb and Thomas Appenzeller. *Sports and the Courts*. The Michie Company, Charlottesville, Virginia, 1980.

Baker, Donald P. "Players Pay for Parents' Values Debate," *The Charlotte Observer,* May 14, 1996.

Benton v. YMCA of Westfield. 136 A 2nd 27 (New Jersey, 1957).

Black, H.C. *H.C. Black's Law Dictionary*. Fourth Edition. West Publishing, St. Paul, Minnesota, 1951.

Carlson, Peter. "Legal Damages." *The Washington Post Magazine*, Washington D.C., p. 12, March 15, 1992.

Dougherty, Neil J., David Auster, Alan Goldberger and Greg Henirmann. *Sport, Physical Activity and the Law*. Human Kinetics, Champaign, Illinois, 1994.

Landers, Ann. "Let's Laugh These Silly Lawsuits Out of Court," *The Charlotte Observer*, Charlotte, North Carolina, p. 8, March 12, 1995.

Lubell, Adele. "Insurance Liability and the American Way of Sport," *The Physician and Sports Medicine*, vol. 15, no. 9, p. 194, September 1987.

Nabozny v. Barnhill, 334 N.E. 2d 258 (Illinois, 1975).

Phay, Robert. "Tort Liability," *Institute of Government*. The University of North Carolina Press, Chapel Hill, North Carolina, 1977.

Random House Webster's College Dictionary. McGraw Hill Edition, New York, New York, 1991.

Stern, R. "Legal Issues in Extracurricular Education," *Nolpe School Law Journal*, vol. 9, 1981.

Swanson v. Wabash College, 504 N.E. 2d 327 (Ohio, 1987).

Verchick, Glenn. "Countering the Criticism of Liebeck v. McDonald's," Queller and Fisher Law Firm, *Internet*, May 21, 1997.

Wong, Glenn. *Essentials of Amateur Sports Law.* Second Edition. Praeger Publishing, Westport, Connecticut, 1994.

Chapter 3

Injuries to Participants

Beyond the winning and the goal, beyond the glory and the flame, he feels the flame within his soul, born of the spirit of the game...

Grantland Rice

Reported injuries to participants in athletic competition goes back at least as far as the "Funeral Games of Achilles" that the blind Greek poet Homer wrote about several thousand years ago in the *Iliad*. In the Roman Coliseum, an injury could lead to a premature and permanent exit from the arena. During the Middle Ages, a knight who was killed during a tournament would have his death ruled a suicide by the Catholic Church and the knight would be excommunicated. Also during the Medieval period, peasants were banned by law from playing football (actually more like soccer) because the numerous injuries kept the peasants from performing their work. In 1905 President Theodore Roosevelt became alarmed at the number of injuries and deaths attributed to college football. In an attempt to save the sport, Roosevelt forced a number of college presidents to come together and form an organization that would clean up football and make it a safer sport. The college presidents formed what became the National Collegiate Athletic Association (N.C.A.A.) and safety in sport still remains one of the priorities of the organization.

Are Injuries Inevitable in Youth Sport?

When people participate in sport there are going to be injuries. According to the United States Consumer Product Safety Commission (C.P.S.C.), there are 58,400 injuries to children each year playing baseball, softball, and tee-ball (*Trial*, 1996). There have been 88 reported deaths of children between the age of 5 and 14, and 61 of the deaths occurred when children were struck by balls, usually in the chest or head.

The National Youth Sports Safety Foundation reports that six children have died in baseball-related injuries since 1994, and since 1979, there have been 21 children to die from soccer goal injuries (Appenzeller and Baron, 1995). From 1989 to 1992 there were 250,000 concussions per year in football, and approximately 650,000 soccer related injuries reported over the same four years. The National Youth Sports Safety Foundation reported that there are an average of 40,000 sports related knee injuries each year. Today we hear about "growth plate" injuries, "little league" elbows, face guards for baseball batting helmets, and flak jackets, as America becomes more concerned about injuries in Youth Sport. With over 25 million participants, the rate of reported injuries is not excessive, but when there are injuries, we are seeing more and more lawsuits alleging negligence as the cause of the injury.

Injuries have always been part of sport, part of the risk of participating in athletic competition. Today when a child is injured playing youth sport, the parent wants to know why. What caused the injury or who caused the injury? Was there lack of proper supervision, unsafe facilities, defective equipment, improper coaching, unfair competition, or a failure to warn about inherent dangers of the activity. Parents want to know, and unfortunately so do many lawyers. This chapter is going to examine some recent cases to look at the difference between winning and losing a lawsuit. To paraphrase Grantland Rice, it does not matter whether you win or lose, but did negligence cause the injury.

Baseball Cases

Lasseigne v. American Legion

On June 3, 1986 Jason Lasseigne was participating in baseball practice for the American Legion Little League team in the Parish of East Baton Rouge (*Lasseigne v. American Legion*, 1990). The practice was held on the wet, grassy playground of Central Middle School after the teams regularly scheduled game had been rained out. Billy Johnson, a father of a team member, volunteered to handle the practice when the regular coach Claude Cassels was unable to attend. During infield practice, Lasseigne was hit on the head with a soggy wet baseball thrown by Todd Landry. Coach Johnson immediately examined Jason and saw no sign of injury, but he did order the youngster to sit out and rest. After a brief rest period, Lasseigne returned to practice where he played shortstop and pitched. Showing no ill effects of the injury, Jason finished practice and Coach Johnson specifically told Lasseigne to inform his parents about what had happened. Jason's mother picked up her son at a friend's house after practice, and she did not notice anything unusual about his behavior and Jason did tell her that he had been hit on the jaw by a baseball. Approximately twenty-four hours later Jason Lasseigne underwent head surgery. Jason's parents filed a lawsuit, individually and on behalf of their son for damages suffered as a result of the injury. The defendants named in the lawsuit were the American Legion Nicholson Post #38; the East Baton Rouge Parish School Board (Controller of the practice field); Claude Cassels and Billy Johnson (team coaches); State Farm Fire and Casualty Company (insurer of Cassels and Johnson under two separate policies); Mr. and Mrs. Jerry Landry (parents of Todd Landry); and Gulf Insurance Company (insurer of Mr. and Mrs. Landry). In the lawsuit the parents made four claims against the defendants:

1. Claude Cassels and Billy Johnson did not adequately supervise the practice.
2. Coaches did not render first aid and assistance to their son as would be expected from an ordinary prudent person in their position.
3. Coaches did not report Jason's injury to them.
4. No one from Post 38 or the coaching staff had ever informed the plaintiffs of the risk that Jason would be taking by participating in baseball (*Lasseigne v. American Legion*, 1990).

In Louisiana, the standard of conduct required of people in their relationships with one another is set forth in Louisiana Civil Code, articles 2315 and 2316:

> Article 2315 provides—Every act whatever of man that causes damages to another obliges him by whose fault it happened to repair it.
> Article 2316 provides—Every person is responsible for the damages he occasions not merely by his act, but by his negligence his imprudence or his want of skill.

The Court of Appeals of Louisiana ruled that Cassels and Johnson acted reasonably under the circumstances present in the case. The court added that reasonable minds could not find the defendants breached their duty of care owed to the plaintiff, and therefore as a matter of law were not liable for the injury. This case brought up issues of supervision, proper medical care, failure to notify of an injury, and failure to warn about possible dangers. The trial court and the court of appeals both ruled that the coaches acted reasonably. However, we know that in sport and physical activity one of the leading causes of lawsuits is lack of follow up by the coaches and administrators. In my opinion, a call from the coach about the extent of Jason's injury would have been better than just telling the player to inform his parents. The coaches did not breach their duty according to the courts, but a personal phone call or visit would have been a better way to communicate. A phone call might have prevented a lawsuit, and saved every one costly legal fees.

Higgins v. Pfeiffer

Jesse Higgins was an amateur baseball player who was struck in the eye by a baseball thrown by a teammate warming up prior to a game (*Higgins v. Pfeiffer*, 1996). Higgins was sitting in the dugout at the time of the accident and he brought a lawsuit against the pitcher who threw the ball; the catcher who signaled for the fast ball, and the acting coach of the team. Higgins and the other members of his team went to the dugout after pregame warmups. Brian Pfeiffer, the pitcher continued to warm up on the sideline by throwing toward the dugout area. As it came closer to game time, catcher, David McCullough, signaled for a rising fast ball which went over the catcher's head and hit Higgins in the eye. Robert McCullough, the acting coach, was charged with negligence for allowing his pitcher to throw toward the dugout. The Appeals Court of Michigan ruled that the plaintiff understood and accepted the dangers of the sport and chose to sit in an area of the dugout that was less protected than the other end, and Higgins failed to pay attention to the activities on the field. The court concluded that the injury sustained was within the scope of plaintiffs consent to participate in the game, and the coach and two teammates were not liable for damages. Higgins understood and accepted the dangers of the sport of baseball, including warm up activities. However, Judge Michael J. Kelly, dissented and he brought up four important points for coaches and administrators to consider:

1. Defendant pitcher was capable of throwing with extreme velocity. Does that make plaintiff's injury foreseeable and a breach of duty of care?
2. All three defendants were aware that the pitcher was throwing toward the dugout and the bench was beginning to fill up. Would a reasonable pitcher and catcher halt the warm up?
3. All three defendants knew that the pitcher would throw his last few warm up pitches as fast as possible. The Head Coach Leonard Makowski testified that the location of the warm up area was unsafe. Should the assistant coach have intervened?
4. Plaintiff had been sitting in the dugout ten to fifteen seconds before being hit. Should the defendants have been aware of plaintiff and reacted accordingly? (*Higgins v. Pfeiffer*, 1996).

Judge Kelly disagreed with the lower court's reliance on the assumption of risk doctrine and stated he would have reversed the decision. Even though Higgins assumed the risk of his injury by participating in the game of baseball, could the injury have been prevented? Probably yes, by moving the pitcher to a safer area, or by making sure players in the dugout were paying attention. There will always be injuries, what we want to do is prevent the unnecessary injuries.

Castro v. Chicago Park District

In *Higgins v. Pfeiffer* the defendants were not liable for the injuries suffered by the player sitting in the dugout. However in *Castro v. Chicago Park District* the opposite decision was handed down. Alex Castro was a Little League player who was hit by a foul ball while seated on the bench during a game. His parents brought a charge of negligence against the Park District, the President of the League and the Team Manager. The parents claimed that the facilities were unsafe and that the defendants were liable. The trial court ruled in favor of the defendants, but the Appellate Court of Illinois reversed the decision. The appellate court held that the baseball league and the President of the League had a duty to supervise and safeguard the participants. The appellate court stated:

> The duties and responsibilities of an organization to which the care and control of children is entrusted are akin to the duties and responsibilities of parents. Such an organization is not an insurer of the safety of children involved. On the other hand, such an organization may not avoid liability for injuries resulting from failure to exercise reasonable care.

The court went on to say:

> The President of the League must be held accountable for the Leagues' activities. A duty voluntarily assumed must be performed with due care or such competence and skill as one possesses. A person can not escape a duty of ordinary care simply because he is a volunteer, particularly where the welfare of children is entrusted to him.

This case is very similar to *Higgins*, yet the decision was very different, and it is harder to control a foul ball than one from a pitcher warming up. In *Higgins*, the court reasoned that the facility was acceptable, in *Castro* it was not. More importantly, the *Castro* decision means that coaches and administrators, whether paid or volunteer, are given the same responsibility for the health, safety, and welfare of the participants as trained and paid coaches. The individual that puts children at risk is liable for any injuries that might result, liability is not based on salary. Coaches and administrators have the responsibility to exercise reasonable care when conducting Youth Sport activities.

Foster v. Houston General Insurance

Robert Foster was a 17-year-old member of a Special Olympic basketball team with an I.Q. of 52 and a mental age of seven years and four months (*Foster v. Houston General Insurance*, 1982). In order to practice for an upcoming tournament, Robert and ten other team members were directed to walk four blocks from their usual outdoor facility to an indoor gymnasium. There were two coaches who were going to supervise the team members on the walk to the indoor facility. Just before they were to leave one of the coaches had a phone call, and the other coach left with the group. On the way to the indoor gym, Robert suddenly ran between two parked cars and was killed. Robert's mother sued the coaches for negligence in the death of her son. The trial court concluded that one coach was not adequate supervision under the circumstances, and Robert's mother was awarded $65,000. The issue in this case was supervision, and the court ruled that the younger the child, chronologically or mentally, and the more dangerous the activity, the greater the need for adequate supervision. The court did not define how many adults would be adequate, but it did rule that 11 members of a Special Olympics team and one adult supervisor was not appropriate. Just as in the *Castro* decision, the Youth League coach and administrator has to assume the responsibility *in loco parentis* (in place of the parents) for the children in their charge. The younger the child, the less risk the child will be able to assume, and the greater responsibility and burden of care that will be placed on the leader. The Youth Sport leader becomes the parent, with the same expectations and responsibilities.

Unforseeable Accidents

Even as a parent, there are still certain injuries that are not preventable. The next case is a tragic example of a young athlete disobeying a directive and suffering a terrible consequence. On June 20, 1985, Ronald Marquez was fatally injured when he fell from the back of a truck that was taking several players to another practice field (Marquez v. Gomez, 1993). Coach Rudy Gonzales and his team had assembled for practice when city park officials asked the team to move to another field. In order to travel about 700 yards the boys were loaded into two vehicles. Coach Gonzales had several team members ride in his Blazer and Phillip Gomez volunteered to give several boys a ride in his truck. The boys riding with Gomez were instructed to ride inside the camper shell on the Ford pick up truck, but three of the boys decided to ride on the rear bumper and hold on to the back of the truck. Ronald Marquez fell off of the truck, managed to get back up and climb back on the vehicle while it was moving. Marquez fell from the truck a second time and died from injuries suffered in the second fall. The parents of the deceased brought a wrongful death action against the driver of the pick up truck, the drivers parents, the baseball coach, and

Little League Baseball, Inc. The district court granted defendants motion for summary judgment and the parents appealed. The plaintiffs charged in their complaint that the coach and Little League Baseball had the responsibility for the safe transportation and physical care of the players, and that the coach negligently supervised the players. Evidence in the case showed that the two vehicles were only going 700 yards on a dirt road without traffic and that the coach gave explicit instructions not to ride on the bumper, but to ride inside the camper top. Rudy Gonzales had been the boys coach for several seasons, and had never had any prior problems with the team members. There was nothing in the record that would lead Coach Gonzales to believe that the young men would disobey his directions. The trial court determined that the accident was not reasonably foreseeable and the Court of Appeals of New Mexico affirmed summary judgment in favor of the coach and Little League Baseball.

Two young men, both going to new practice facilities, were tragically killed. In one case, supervision was adequate, in the other it was inadequate, leading to a finding of negligence. The biggest difference was the age and experience of the two players. Robert Foster had a mental age of seven years and four months while Ronald Marquez was an average teenager. One coach, giving specific instructions was adequate, one coach with a Special Olympics team was not adequate. These two cases demonstrate that a reasonably prudent person shall understand their athletes that he or she is in charge of and adjusts accordingly.

Out-of-Court Settlements

When Youth Sport cases go to court, a judge and or a judge and jury decides whether there was negligence, and whether the Youth Sport leaders acted as reasonable prudent people. What happens when the case is settled out-of-court? Out-of-court settlements create no common law, no guidelines for others to follow, no do's and don'ts. In out-of-court settlements we are exposed to issues, but there is no resolution, just a monetary agreement. Let me report two significant out-of-court settlements, and the issues these cases raise for Youth Sport leaders. Joey Fort was a ten-year-old Little League second baseman who was selected for the All-Star Team in Rumenede, New Jersey (Blodegett, 1986). For post-season competition, Joey was moved to the outfield where during practice he lost a pop fly in the sun and suffered an injury to his eye. The Forts sued the two volunteer Little League Coaches for $750,000 on behalf of their son. The parents claimed that the coaches were negligent, because they had failed to instruct their son in how to use his glove to shield his eyes from the sun. The plaintiffs also charged that if the coaches were not going to teach Joey how to shade his eyes, then they should have given him flip-up sun glasses, like they wear in the Major Leagues. The coaches settled the case out of court for $25,000 and the settlement had a drastic affect on Youth Sport in Rumenede, and in the entire state of New Jersey. After the settlement, it was almost impossible for Youth Sport Organizations to find volunteer coaches, and many activities stopped. The State of New Jersey in 1986 and amended in 1988 passed the "Little League Liability Law" to protect volunteer coaches. The New Jersey Legislation will be discussed in another area, but the key issue of the Fort case is that volunteer coaches were being sued for not teaching proper technique. Since the case did not go to court, we do not know if the coaches were held negligent or not, we just know what the issues were.

Lloyd v. Jewish Community Center

The other significant out-of-court settlement was *Lloyd v. Jewish Community Center*. Adam Lloyd was a 14-year-old swim team member practicing at the Jewish Community Center in Montgomery County, Maryland. Adam's coach told him to begin swimming laps, so Adam did a pike dive off of the starting blocks into the shallow end of the pool, and crushed his spine, rendering him a quadriplegic (*Atlanta Law Reporter*, 1986). The parents sued the Jewish Community Center, the Swim Team Coaches, and United States Swimming, Inc. for improper coaching and training, failure to warn, and failure to supervise. The case was settled out-of-court

for $4.1 million dollars. A 14-year-old teenager does a pike dive in 3.5 feet of water, a tragedy, but was there negligence? The case was settled, but the issues remain, improper coaching, failure to warn, and failure to supervise; what was done, and what if anything should have been done? What did happen was that United States Swimming, Inc. recommended that all starting blocks be moved to the deep end of the pool, not the shallow end.

These cases demonstrate that Youth Sport coaches and administrators have the same legal responsibilities toward their athletes as parents have toward their child. Whether or not the coach or administrator is paid or a volunteer has no bearing on the duty owed to the participants. The Youth Sport leader has to be a reasonable prudent person when assuming the responsibility of the safety of children.

After the Facts

Of Parents and Sports and Harold

A few weeks ago in Huntington Beach, Calif., an angry parent rushed out of the bleachers during a Senior League baseball game and allegedly decked a 16-year-old umpire for a call that had allowed his son's opposing team to score a run.

Recently in El Centro, Calif., the final eight games of a Little League season were canceled after another so-called adult jumped out of the stands and threatened an umpire with a knife. The ballplayers in question were 8-year-olds.

You hear these stories and realize that nothing really changes, that too often the games of children are played for adults. It was that way 20 years ago and probably 40 before that.

We all knew kids in Little League or Pop Warner football who kept one eye on the ball and one on the stands. We've heard stories of sons who played $20-a-homer with their dads. We all felt the aching tug in our stomachs when the bases were loaded and we were at bat.

It can be serious business, being a kid, especially for the ones who don't want to be out there in the first place.

Whenever I hear stories about kids and parents and sports, I can't help but think of a boy named Harold. Sometimes I'll think of him when passing a ballfield.

Harold was one of my teammates on a midget Pop Warner team in North Orange County, Calif. We were eighth-graders.

I didn't know him well, but I do know that Harold had no business playing football.

I didn't know his parents and can't begin to question their motives. I can't tell you why, or even if they pushed their son out of the car every day for practice. As an eighth-grader with glowing red hair and swizzle sticks for legs, I had my own problems.

What I remember most about Harold is the sight of him crying. He cried almost every day.

Harold was a bona fide clod. His uniform hung on him like an over-sized suit. He made a clanking sound when he ran. His pants drooped in the seat, and his thigh pads roamed around his upper legs, protecting everything but his thighs.

Tucked inside his helmet, Harold sort of looked like a puffer fish. When he bit into his mouthpiece, his eyes popped opened wide and his cheeks filled with air.

When we ran wind sprints, Harold cried. When we crawled up the dirt hill behind out practice field, Harold cried. When we had tackling drills, Harold cried even more.

We, of course, handled Harold with all the tact of eighth-graders. We knocked him around like a pinball. He was an easy target, and no matter how bad you were, you always looked better after tackling Harold.

When Harold cried, we laughed. With collective wit we reminded him daily that crying was for babies, not for someone so close to puberty.

That all changed one day.

There's a tackling drill in football in which two players lie flat on their backs about 10 yards apart. One player holds a ball. At the whistle, the players jump to their feet and run toward each other like two locomotives locked on the same track.

I had a good view when Harold and a guy named Jim took their places on the ground. I was next in line to tackle.

Harold held the ball against his stomach. The whistle blew, and Harold ran toward Jim.

Jim hit him hard, helmet to helmet. We all cheered.

Harold didn't. Of course, he cried. Our coach ordered Harold to his feet and told him a few laps would shake the cobwebs from his head.

Harold took two steps and dropped to the ground.

Our coach cradled him in his arms, but Harold wouldn't move. His eyes were wide open, but they refused to blink.

I had never seen anyone die before.

We were ordered to run circles around the field for no other reason that to keep us from staring. We ran for what seemed like hours, watching as they finally carried Harold off the field to the hospital.

The next day, someone explained to us how a blood clot had formed in Harold's brain and that the blow to his head was fatal.

Jim wasn't there to hear it.

We gathered as a team and, for some reason, voted to continue the season. Some of our mothers begged us to quit, but the only one who did was Jim.

We went to the funeral and went on with our lives. But most of us will never forget what happened that day. I hope I remember long enough to tell a son of mine.

Recently, I drove past my old Little League field and watched as one youngster took his position in right field. I wondered if he really wanted to be there.

Sometimes I'll think of Harold and wonder what might have become of him. He might have been a great lawyer or an accountant. Maybe a space scientist.

We all know he couldn't play football. But, then again, he never said he could (St. Louis Post-Dispatch, 1986).

References

Appenzeller, H. And R. Baron. *From the Gym to the Jury*, Greensboro, North Carolina, vol. 7, no. 2, 1995.

Blodgett, N. *ABA Journal the Lawyers Magazine*, February 1986.

Castro v. Chicago Park District. 533 N.E. 2d 504 (Illinois, 1988).

Community Center. "Coach Liability," *Atlanta Law Reporter*, Atlanta, Georgia, 1987.

Dufresne, Chris. "Of Parents and Sports and Harold," *St. Louis Post-Dispatch*, July 24, 1986.

Foster v. Houston General Insurance Company, 407 So. 2d 759 (Texas, 1982).

Higgins v. Pfeiffer, 546 N.W. 2d 645 (Michigan, 1996).

Lasseigne v. American Legion, 558 So. 2d. 614 (Louisiana, 1990).

Lloyd v. Jewish Community Center, Montgomery Circuit Court No. 0260 (Maryland, 1986).

Marquez v. Gomez, 866 P 2d. 354 (New Mexico, 1993).

News and Trends, *Trial*, August 1996.

Walton, G. *Beyond Winning*. Leisure Press, Champaign, Illinois, 1992.

Chapter 4

Injuries Caused by Participants

A reckless disregard for the safety of other players can not be excused.

Nabozny v. Barnhill

What happens when an athlete gets injured in the arena, during practice or game, and the injury is caused by another player? Today in a lawsuit, we want to know who is to blame. Coaches traditionally carry the burden of protecting participants from injury. Historically, when athletes played a game, they assumed the risk of injury. In the last twenty years we have begun to see injured athletes suing the participant who might have caused the injury.

Player on Player Injuries

Soccer: *Nabozny v. Barnhill*

That old saying, "all is fair in love and war," is not true in sport any more. In 1975 a landmark case changed forever how we view players responsibility to each other (*Nabozny v. Barnhill*, 1975). Julian Nabozny was a goal keeper at Duke Child's Field in Winnetka, Illinois when he went down on his left knee to receive a pass, pulled the ball into his chest, and was kicked on the left side of the head by David Barnhill, a member of the opposing team. Nabonzy's father brought a tort action against Barnhill to recover damages for personal injury caused by the negligence of the defendant. The soccer match was played under "F.I.F.A." rules, which prohibits all players from making contact with the goal keeper when he is in possession of the ball in the penalty area. Under F.I.F.A. rules, any contact with a goal keeper in possession of the ball in the penalty area is an infraction of the rules, even if the contact is unintentional. The only legal contact permitted in soccer is shoulder to shoulder contact between players going for a ball within playing distance. The defendant claimed that a player should be immune from tort action for any injury that happens during the course of a game and the Circuit Court of Cook County directed a verdict in favor of Barnhill. The trial court ruled that Nabozny assumed the risk of injury when he decided to play in the game. The Appellate Court of Illinois reversed and remanded the decision of the circuit court stating:

> This court believes that the law should not place unreasonable burdens on the free and vigorous participation in sports by our youth. However, we also believe that organized athletic competition does not exist in a vacuum. Rather, some of the restraints of civilization must accompany every athlete onto the playing field. One of the educational benefits of organized athletic competition to our youth is the development of discipline and self control (Nabozny, 1975).

The court went on to add: "A player then is charged with a legal duty to every other player on the field to refrain from conduct proscribed by a safety rule. A reckless disregard for the safety of other players can not be excused." In the opinion of the court, a player is liable for injury in a tort action if his conduct is such that it is either deliberate, willful, or with reckless disregard for the safety of the other player. Nabozny is a landmark decision in sport because it means that athletes do not have to tolerate or accept the behavior of competitors that violate the rules of the game. There is no place in sport for the cheap shot artist, the individual who's goal is to injure or to inflict pain on opposing players. Assumption of Risk means that players will obey the rules, and if an injury happens, it happens.

Hockey: *Overall v. Kadella*

In the case of *Overall v. Kadella* an action was brought by a young man who was struck in the eye during a fight following a hockey match. On April 17, 1975 two amateur hockey teams, the Waterford Lakers and the Clarkston Flyers engaged in a contest. At the conclusion of the match, a fight broke out, both benches cleared and a melee resulted. Randall Overall, the plaintiff, remained on the bench during the fight, but Steven Kadella, the defendant, skated over and struck the plaintiff with his hockey stick knocking the young man unconscious and fracturing the bones around his right eye. The hockey referees testified that Kadella engaged in at least three separate fights after the game was over and he was given three game misconducts. Fighting is against the rules of the Michigan Amateur Hockey Association, and the intent of the rule is to prevent violence. The trial court found that Overall had suffered damages of $21,000 for out-of-pocket expenses, pain and suffering, and permanent injury. He was awarded an additional $25,000 because the defendant's act had been intentional and malicious. On appeal, Kadella contended that the plaintiff could not sue for an injury when the plaintiff was a volunteer participant, using the phrase:

'*Volenti non fit injuria*' (he who consents can not receive an injury.)

The court of appeals held that the defendant's intentional battery certainly violated the leagues rules against fighting and the defendant was held liable for the injuries sustained by the plaintiff. The court added:

> Participation in a game involves a manifestation of consent to those bodily contacts which are permitted by the rules of the game. However, there is general agreement that an intentional act causing injury which goes beyond what is ordinarily permissible, is an assault and battery for which recovery may be had (*Overall v. Kabella*, 1984).

Violations of safety rules which lead to injuries will not be acceptable today in Youth Sport. Deliberately trying to inflict pain or injury is not part of the game.

Basketball: *Griggas v. Clauson*

Basketball is a contact sport today and one of the first cases of too much contact goes back to 1955. Robert Griggas, in an action by his mother, sued LaVerne Clauson for damages that resulted from injuries suffered in a basketball game (*Griggas v. Clauson*, 1955). Robert was a member of the Rockford Athletic Club, while LaVerne played for the Blackhawk Athletic Club when the confrontation took place. The plaintiff charged that during the game, while his back was turned, the defendant hit him on the head and knocked him unconscious. Griggas suffered lacerations, abrasions, contusions, concussions, temporary and permanent injuries, and the loss of a four-year college scholarship. The trial court awarded the plaintiff $2,000 in damages on the assault and battery action against Clauson. Assault and battery is not part of the game, not part of the risks that are assumed when playing basketball. The $2,000 award for damages does not seem very much when considering the severity of the injuries that Robert suffered. However, in 1955 the hospital bill came to $262.10 and the doctor's bill was $100.00. The balance, after paying the medical expenses, would have been $1,637.90, a substantial amount for that day. What Clauson did violated the rules of the game of basketball, and he was held liable for the damages that resulted from his conduct. Inappropriate action on the court or field is not acceptable.

Baseball: *Gaspard v. Grain Dealers*

Ronnie Gaspard was an 11-year-old youngster when he was struck by a bat that slipped through the hands of 12-year-old Ronald Viator (*Gaspard v. Grain Dealers*, 1961). Gaspard's parents sued Viator's parents and Grain Dealer Mutual Insurance Company, the insurer of the defendant. Viator was the batter and Gaspard was 15 feet behind the batter, stooping to select his own bat, when a pitch was made, Viator swung, the bat slipped and hit the plaintiff on the head. Both boys were voluntary participants in the baseball game, it was a supervised athletic contest and both boys testified that they had played before and since the accident. The plaintiffs argued that the 12-year-old defendant was negligent for batting with Gaspard so near by, and for using a heavy bat. The court concluded that the Viator youth was not negligent, in fact he exercised that degree of care reasonably expected from a boy of his age playing the sport of baseball. The court added that the only thing Viator could have done to prevent the injury was to not bat. According to appeals court Judge Culpepper, "to impose liability under these circumstances, would render the participation of children in almost every game or sport a practical impossibility and would be a constant nightmare for parents." The court of appeals affirmed the trial court ruling denying recovery for the plaintiff based on the assumption of risk doctrine. The trial court held that:

> it appears that generally a participant in a lawful game or contest assumes the danger inherent in that game or contest with consequent preclusion from recovery for injury or death resulting therefrom.
> But he does not assume the risk of injury resulting from negligence. Nor does the voluntary participant assume the extraordinary risks of the game or contest unless he knew of them and voluntarily assented to them (*Gaspard v. Grain Dealers*, 1961).

Another important point of law to come out of this case is that children are not expected to conform to the standard of behavior that is expected of an adult. Children are to be judged by the standard of behavior of other children of the same age, intelligence, and experience. In this situation there were no safety rules violated, and therefore the defendant was not liable for the injuries to the plaintiff. Both young men voluntarily participated in the game and both knew the inherent risk of the sport, both chose to play and both assumed the risk of injury. If this case happened today, the coach could have been named a defendant for not making sure the plaintiff was far enough away to escape injury from the bat. It appears that unless the batter intentionally threw the bat out of anger or frustration, the batter would still not be held liable today for this injury.

Softball: *Novak v. Lamar*

In a 1986 softball case, the difference between assumption of risk and unsportsmanlike conduct is emphasized. John Novak was a first baseman playing in a church league run by the Monroe Recreation Department in Monroe, Louisiana (*Novak v. Lamar*, 1966). A ball was hit to the infield, a poor throw to first base caused Novak to come off the base where he was hit in the face by the base runner. The trial court found that Novak had played baseball and softball for several years, knew the dangers of playing first base, and had been taught to come off the base on the infield side. Evidence was admitted that Novak did not come off the base on the infield side, and the base runner did nothing illegal or unsportsmanlike. The trial court held:

> The situation was simply an inherent part of the game, and both players assumed the risk of just such a collusion if they played the game competitively and with maximum diligence (*Novak v. Lamar*, 1966).

The Court of Appeals in Louisiana found that the base runner did not act in an unexpected or unsportsmanlike way with reckless lack of concern for Novak. The injury was part of the game, part of normal play, was not the result of a safety rule violation, and therefore the player assumed the risk of such an injury when he decided to play the game. The first baseman had actually been taught how to avoid a collision and failed to execute the correct technique. If the base runner had gone out of the base path or had deliberately attempted to hurt the first baseman, the decision could have been different. Playing by the rules, playing hard and competitively, but still following the rules of the sport is the best policy for participants.

Bowling: *Gamble v. Bost*

In a very unusual case, in fact the first of its kind that I have found, legal action was brought against an 11-year-old bowler. On December 6, 1987 Lisa Gamble and her husband Kevin were guests at Marriott's Tan-Tar-A-Resort at the Lake of the Ozarks (*Gamble v. Bost*, 1995). The couple was bowling at the Resorts Bowling Alley, sitting at the scorers table when Lisa was hit in the head by a bowling ball thrown by Travis Bost. The ball apparently slipped out of Bost's hand while he was testing it, hit a railing, and then struck Gamble causing injuries to Lisa's head and jaw. Gamble filed a civil suit against Bost and Marriott, alleging negligence of the child and liability of the owners of the bowling alley. A jury verdict found in favor of the defendants, but Gamble filed a motion for a new trial. The Circuit Court of Boone County granted a new trial motion as to the child, but denied the new trial motion against Marriott. Gamble and Bost both appealed. The court of appeals affirmed the new trial against Bost and reversed the no new trial decision against Marriott. Missouri case law holds to a reckless standard for injuries arising out of participation in athletic competition:

> personal injuries incurred during athletic competition must be predicated as recklessness not mere negligence (*Gamble v. Bost*, 1995).

However, bowling does not allow contact between participants and being hit in the head by a bowling ball is not the usual type of injury associated with the sport. The court held that there was no burden on participation in bowling by using the negligence standard and that Bost owed a duty of ordinary care to Gamble. According to Prosser, and Keeton on Torts, the defense of assumption of risk is based on several elements:

> First, the person must know that the risk is present and he must understand its nature, and second his choice to participate must be free and voluntary. . .
> Under normal circumstances the person will not be taken to assume any risk of either activities or conditions of which there is no knowledge. The person must know the facts that create the danger, and be able to appreciate and comprehend the nature of the danger (*Gamble v. Bost*, 1995).

The evidence in this case demonstrated that the bowling ball was launched with sufficient force to travel to the scorer's table and hit people seated five to six feet from the rail. Common sense as to how bowling balls are usually tested means that it would be up to a jury to determine if there was negligence on the part of Bost. A directed verdict by the trial court in favor of Bost would not have been appropriate. The court of appeals remanded the case back to the trial court to allow a jury to determine if Bost was negligent in his actions. The standard of care for participants in contact sports is different from the accepted standard of care in non-contact sports. For contact sports there has to be a reckless disregard by one participant for the health and safety of another participant. In a non-contact sport the mere evidence of negligence by a participant may be sufficient for a cause of action. Negligent conduct in a non-contact sport is a question for a jury to decide. *Gamble v. Bost* establishes a different standard of care for contact sport versus non-con-

tact sports. Injuries are more acceptable to participants who voluntarily consent to participate in sporting events where the chance of injury is greater and expected.

Tackle Football

There are two other cases that involve lawsuits between participants in informal games and these two cases help to clarify the Doctrine of Assumption of Risk. Vance Kabella through his mother filed a lawsuit against Greg Bouschelle seeking damages for injuries sustained in a game of tackle football (*Kabella v. Bouschelle*, 1983). The complaint alleged that during the game Bouschelle threw Kabella to the ground while making a tackle, causing Kabella to suffer a dislocated hip. The civil suit claims that Bouschelle breached his duty of care to Kabella, subjected him to unreasonable risk of harm, and asked for a total of $107,310.28 for personal injuries, pain and suffering, and medical expenses. At issue was whether a participant in an athletic activity involving physical contact between players may recover in tort for the alleged negligent conduct of another participant. In *Kuehner v. Green* 436 So. 2d. 78 (1983), Justice Boyd noted:

> Historically, the courts have been reluctant to allow persons to recover money damages for injuries received while participating in a sport, especially a contact sport, unless there was a deliberate attempt to injure.

Reckless Misconduct

Reckless misconduct means that a choice is made, a course of action taken that is dangerous and that the danger of the action is known to a reasonable person. Players in informal sandlot games do not have the benefit of written rules, coaches, referees, or instant replay to supervise or evaluate player action. Unless there is an intentional tort or reckless conduct, then there is no course of action. There have to be rules and controls to protect players, but at the same time if there is a constant fear of a civil lawsuit, people will not be able to play the game properly. Voluntary consent to participate means accepting the normal risks that go when bodily contact is permitted under the rules and there is then an assumption of risk when injuries happen from simply playing the sport. Backyard football and basketball, or pick up baseball games are common activities for today's youth. These activities are difficult to monitor and participants have to assume the risk if they are injured during normal play.

Backyard Games

The next case, again demonstrates an over reaction to a backyard contest. Thirty years ago this case would, in all probability, never have come to trial, but today's climate is different. Robert Keller was 14-years-old and playing a goalie in a game of floor hockey when he was struck in the eye by a plastic puck shot by 13-year-old Ralph Mols, Jr. (*Keller v. Mols*, 1987). In the lawsuit the plaintiffs claimed that Mols was negligent for shooting the hockey puck in the direction of the goalie who was not wearing protective equipment, and the parents were negligent for allowing the children to play on their property and for failing to warn the children about the dangers of the sport and playing without protective equipment. The trial court held that participants were involved in a contact sport and that players would not be liable for injuries unless there was willful and wanton conduct. The trial court and the appeals court both agreed that there was no evidence to support the claim of intentional or reckless disregard for the safety of the participants. Here we have a backyard case that is heard on the circuit court level and then appealed and for three years ties up the legal system. Fortunately, the circuit court and court of appeals used common sense in handing down their decisions, but we will probably continue to see more of this type of litigation in the future.

Violence in Sport

In the United States today, there is a growing concern about violence in sport. Player violence has become an issue in the National Hockey

League, the National Football League, Major League Baseball, and the National Basketball Association. Drugs, societal issues, sport issues, and violence received much attention recently when Mike Tyson bit Evander Holyfield's ear. The cases we have examined reflect that concern, the belief that even in contact and collusion sport there are still standards of acceptable behavior. The Gladiatorial contests of ancient Rome may not have had any rules, but it is the rules of the game that has established modern sport as one of the civilizing agents of society. The athlete who crosses over the line may find himself suspended or banished and now that athlete is also open for personal litigation. Most sports today have established safety rules to help define the line between what is legal and illegal behavior on the playing field (Wong, 1994). Safety rules are designed to protect the participants and prevent injuries, and the establishment of a safety rule creates a legal duty owed by the player to the other participants. It is critical that Youth Sport coaches explain and teach the rules of the sport, encourage players to abide by the rules, and discipline those who violate the rules.

Coach's Liability

Coaches who encourage wrongful acts and players that commit these acts may be held liable for the damages their actions create. Players have an obligation to abide by the rules and coaches have an obligation to teach the rules. The "win at all cost" mentality is not acceptable if it puts the health and safety of others in jeopardy. Unfortunately the Tysons, Alomars, and Rodmans of the professional leagues have done a disservice to sport that the youth leagues will have to try and correct. Play hard, play fair, play within the rules should be the motto for Youth Sport.

After the Facts

Baseball's Head First Slide

With the score tied 4–4 in the bottom of the 7th, the Dentsville American Legion team had a rally going. Joey White, Dentsville's runner at second, got the steal sign and took off for third.

"I remember thinking, 'Should I go in head first or feet first?'" Joey recalled Monday. "It's a little bit more deceiving for the umpire to make the call when you go in head first, that's what the coaches always said."

So Joey dove headlong into third—and changed his whole life.

The 17-year-old, already a college and professional baseball prospect, slammed his head into the third baseman's knee, shatter-

ing the sixth vertebra in his neck and leaving him paralyzed, perhaps permanently.

"My head was laying on the dirt and all I could see was my hand in front of my face," Joey said, lying in his hospital bed at Richland Memorial Hospital. "I remember just thinking of what life would be like in a wheelchair."

In the two weeks since, Joey has been flat on his back, his head held rigid by weights and pulleys. He can use his arms and hands but has little feeling from his chest down.

Baseball isn't usually thought of as a dangerous sport, but Joey is the eighth American player since 1982 — all high school age — to be permanently disabled during a game. Using the slide Pete Rose helped make famous, three or four were hurt diving head first, said UNC-Chapel Hill physical education Professor Fred Mueller, a national authority on sports injuries.

And because of Joey's injury, state and national officials with American Legion baseball will be discussing changing the rules about sliding, said Joe Clayton, the South Carolina American Legion baseball director.

"We've never talked about (banning headfirst slides) before, but we're talking about it now," said Clayton, who said national officials are aware of White's injury.

There have been 80 permanently disabling injuries in football since 1982, 75% of them broken necks, Mueller said.

Almost 11 million college and high school students have played football and 3.2 million have played baseball since 1982, when Mueller first began keeping statistics.

There have been previous efforts to reduce injuries—even talk of prohibiting headfirst slides.

Since a North Carolina high school catcher suffered a broken neck blocking a base runner at home plate a few years ago, North Carolina high school rules have required that runners slide, rather than try to knock opponents down.

But no one has outlawed diving for a base—a part of baseball for more than 100 years. The idea was discussed at a national high school federation meeting in Kansas City recently, UNC's Mueller said, but nothing came of it.

Mueller said a headfirst slide shouldn't be dangerous so long as the player keeps his head up. Joey's coach Bruce Smalley attributed the tragedy to a comibnation of Joey's technique and a freak accident, although Joey remembers following the rules.

Joey's mother, Kaye White, said, "Everything had to happen exactly the way it did, in an nth of second. If you tried to stage something like that, you couldn't."

Joey's father, Frank, who was announcing the game from the press box, said he watched the third baseman field a wide throw from the catcher, bobble the ball and turn to pick up the ball and meet the runner.

"Joey was coming in, and the top of his head went into the boy's knee," Frank White said. "And because his cleats were dug in, of course, there was no give."

On Monday, Joe was scheduled to show off his pitching and hitting to Atlanta Braves scouts, who had invited him to Sumter to try-out with other prospects for the next year's draft.

A rising senior at Richland Northeast High School, he had also attracted the interest of college coaches at Duke, Florida State and the University of Tennessee.

"His tremendous, intense competitive nature made him as good as he was..." said Smalley. "He hadn't come close to reaching his potential."

Joey's goals are different now. Friends say the family has insurance to cover the bills for now—although lifetime care for a permanently disabled person can cost hundreds of thousands of dollars.

"My dream would be to walk, but if that doesn't come, I just want a family," he said.

His hospital room already is filled with mementos:

There is a red-and-blue Dentsville baseball cap with Joey's number 16 added to one side, which the team is wearing for the rest of the season.

There is the prom picture, taken May 18, with Joey in white tie and tails, and his girlfriend, Sabrina Pitts, in a red formal dress.

And there is a photo of Joey's car, the maroon 1951 Chevy his father bought for his 16th birthday last year.

He plans to sell it.

"It's a straight shift, and I've got to go to hand controls," Joey said (Eichel, n.d.).

References

Eichel, Henry. "Baseball's Head First Slide: Ban Pondered After Teen Breaks Neck," *The State Newspaper*.

Gamble v. Bost, 901 S.W. 2d. 182 (Missouri, 1995).

Gaspard v. Grain Dealers Mutual Insurance Company, 132 So. 2d. 831 (Louisiana, 1961).

Griggas v. Clauson, 128 N.E. 2d. 363 (Illinois, 1955).

Kabella v. Bouschelle, 672 P. 2d. 290 (New Mexico, 1983).

Keller v. Mols, 509 N.E. 2d 584 (Illinois, 1987).

Kuehner v. Green, 436 S. 2nd. 78 (1983).

Nabozny v. Barnhill, 334 N.E. 2d 258 (Illinois, 1975).

Novak v. Lamar Ins. Co., 488 So. 2d 739 (Louisiana, 1986).

Overall v. Kabella, 361 N.W. 2d. 352 (Michigain, 1984).

Wong, Glenn. *Essentials of Amateur Sport*. Second Edition. Praeger, Westport, Connecticut, 1994.

Chapter 5

Injuries to Spectators

"Panis et Circus"
(Bread and Games)

On May 6, 1995, eight-year-old Johnny Lupoli was warming up before a baseball game in Wallingford, Connecticut (*Sports Illustrated*, 1996). Johnny, a pitcher for the Kovacs Insurance team in the Yalesville Little League overthrew his catcher during the pre-game session and hit a spectator. Carol LaRosa, the injured spectator, who's son was a teammate of Lupoli, sued the young pitcher for $15,000 in damages. According to the lawsuit, LaRosa suffered cuts requiring stitches, permanent injuries causing jaw and joint pain, and general nervous shock (Wong, 1997). LaRosa and her husband Thomas claimed damages for negligence and loss of consortium in naming Lupoli as the sole defendant. New Haven Superior Court Judge Ronald J. Fracosse dismissed the lawsuit because the minor was the only defendant and the complaint was not served on a parent or next friend (LaRosa, 1997). The State Appellate Court reversed the decision of the superior court, and ruled that the Wallingford mother could sue the Little Leaguer and that the defendant's motion to dismiss was improperly granted. The LaRosa's attorney Joseph DeLucia in explaining the lawsuit stated:"Lawsuits are a search for truth" (*Sports Illustrated*, 1996). An eight-year-old Little Leaguer got sued for $15,000 because he overthrew his catcher during warm ups and a spectator was injured.

Spectators

Spectators at sporting events are like fireworks on the Fourth of July, part of the reason we have athletic events, part of the sporting tradition. It is the crowd that helps create the excitement of the contest, that drives the contestants. We have had spectators at sporting events for as long as we have had contests. Homer, writing in the *Iliad* about the funeral games of Patroclus, describes early spectators: "Achilles held the troops upon the spot and seated them forming a wide arena" (Swanson, 1995). The ancient

Greeks enjoyed watching the festivals and early Olympic games, although historians believe that the spectators were limited to males only. It has been suggested that female spectators would be killed if discovered. *"Panis et Circus"* describes the Roman attitude of Bread and Circuses, a philosophy used to pacify the masses. The Romans built huge spectator oriented facilities such as the Coliseum and Circus Maximus to entertain the vast numbers of unemployed in Rome and other cities. In the Roman sports facilities, there were box seats for the important and wealthy citizens and women were allowed to attend events, but were required to sit in segregated areas. Augustus Caesar had a ten foot wide, ten foot deep canal dug in one of the arenas, then filled with water, so that spectators would be protected when wild beasts were exhibited. We can see the canal as a Roman attempt at risk management strategy, to put on the event, but try to reduce the chance of danger to the spectators. Today it is more important than ever that we protect spectators when they are attending sporting events. Accidents and injuries to spectators means lawsuits, and cases involving injured spectators at Youth Sport Activities goes back to the days of World War II.

Soap Box Derbies

In 1941 William H. Murphy and Sarah Dargel sued the Jarvis Chevrolet Company, the *Peoria Journal Transcript, Inc.*, and Johnson's Sales and Services, to recover for injuries when they were struck by a momentum propelled home made automobile, engaged in a Soap Box Derby race (*Murphy v. Jarvis*, 1941). The plaintiffs claimed that the defendants were negligent for failing to erect and maintain a barrier between the track and the spectators. The jury ruled that the sponsors were not negligent and that the spectators were contributorily negligent. However, the appellate court reversed the judgment of the lower court.

Protecting Invitees

Another Soap Box Derby case occurred in 1951 when John Bango, a police officer was injured during the race (*Bango v. Carteret Lions Club*, 1951). A 13-year-old male contestant lost control of his car, veered off course, and ran into the plaintiff. The Superior Court of New Jersey held: "a person who entices others to come upon his premises is under a duty to exercise reasonable care for their protection." The Superior Court added:

> in order that the defendants be liable, it must be shown that they had such a degree of control that they could have averted the danger, or such superior knowledge that they should have foreseen and given

warning of a danger not apparent to the Plaintiff (*Bango v. Carteret Lions Club*, 1951).

The defendants, Carteret Lions Club, sponsored the Soap Box Derby, but the appellate court ruled that sponsorship did not give the Lions Club control of the race track. The Lions Club delegated the protection of the spectators over to the Police and Fire Departments, thus fulfilling their obligation to the public. The appellate court found that the Lions Club was not liable for the failure of the Police and Fire Departments to take proper precautions. In this situation, the Carteret Lions Club met their responsibility to protect the spectators by delegating out security to two other organizations (*Bango v. Carteret Lions Club*, 1951). However, in *Watford v. Evening Star Newspaper Company*, the court's decision was the opposite (*Watford v. Evening Star*, 1954). The *Evening Star Newspaper Company* sponsored the Washington Soap Box Derby for boys age 11 to 15. The boys built miniature race cars and competed for prizes, spectators were admitted free of charge, and the event and its sponsors were extensively publicized. The race was held on public property and arrangements were made to have police supervise the event. Herman Watford was a six-year-old spectator who was injured when the car of a 12-year-old driver went out of control and crashed into the crowd. The United States Court of Appeals held:

> Whenever one invites others to come up on property for the purpose of viewing or participating in an event which was set in motion and is conducted for some private purpose or benefit, those invited have a right to assume not only that the sponsor has the authority to use the property for that purpose and that the sponsor has the ability to protect the invitees from foreseeable dangers (*Watford v. Evening Star*, 1954).

If the sponsor fails to provide the appropriate safety measures, then the sponsor may be held liable for any injuries that result. The court of appeals added: "liability to invitees is not imposed merely because of ownership but because of the invitation (*Watford v. Evening Star*, 1954). When the public is invited to an event, to a youth sport game, that invitation creates a relationship, and that relationship gives rise to a duty. The appellate court concluded: "a spectator at a Soap Box Derby race should be able to assume that the promoters have taken reasonable caution for the safety of the spectators and calling in the police does not automatically discharge the duty" (*Watford v. Evening Star*, 1954).

Two similar cases, two different decisions regarding the liability of the sponsoring organizations and their duty to protect the spectators. I believe that the biggest difference in these two cases is the age of the plaintiffs. John Bango was a police officer assigned to the race, while Herman Watford was a six-year-old child. Not knowing the seriousness of the injuries, the police officer's case seems frivolous on the surface, while the six-year-old seems tragic. Justice may be blind, but emotion and sympathy still factor in many decisions. If these same two cases happened today, the Sponsors, the Police, Fire Departments, Recreation Department, City Hall, and the County Commissioners would probably all be named as defendants in the lawsuit. Both cases demonstrate that when people attend an event, a game, a race, there is an expectation of security and safety that comes with the invitation.

In the case of *Christianson v. Hager* two spectators become involved in a pushing and shoving match at a baseball game. The defendant, Hager made a threat against the health and welfare of the umpire, and Christianson defended the man in black and he was thrown over a fence. Christianson took action against Hager for assault and against the Recreation Association for failure to supervise the crowd properly. The jury ruled that the defendant did not commit assault and if there was no assault, then there was no case against the Recreation Association. The Supreme Court of Minnesota agreed with the lower court ruling that since no assault and battery had been committed against the plaintiff, there could be no recovery against the Recreation Association. However, the Supreme Court of Minnesota added: "the proprietor of a place of amusement has the duty to protect patrons from negligent injury at the hands of others as well as from injury resulting from intentional torts committed by other patrons" (*Christianson v. Hager*, 1954). Even though this decision favored the Recreation Association, the theme emerges that owners and operators of recreational facilities have a duty to protect spectators from injuries.

Mann v. Nutrilite: Failure to Warn of Danger

Gene Mann was a chaperone for a girls softball team called the Pirates. During a warm up period she was standing in the outfield and was hit by a ball (*Mann v. Nutrilite*, 1955). Mann sought damages for her injuries from four defendants, Nutrilite Product, Inc., Nutrilite Foundations, B.P. Kids, Inc., and Boys Club of Oceana Park. The plaintiff claimed that the corporations owned and operated the Pirates, and that the girl Bessie Baker, who threw the ball, was an agent of the corporations. Mann alleged that Baker negligently and unlawfully threw the softball and that the defendants negligently and unlawfully trained and managed her. B.P. Kids was a nonprofit corporation that promoted Youth activities in Oceana Park, and the Pirates were a softball team for girls under the age of 18. The Nutrilite Corporation as a sponsor had the word "Nutrilite" sewn on the back of the uniforms. The appellate court held:

A person does not assume the risk of another person's negligent conduct but in this case there was no substantial evidence of negligence on the part of Baker. Since there was no evidence that ordinary care was not exercised by management, spectator assumed the risk of injury (*Mann v. Nutrilite*, 1955).

During the proceedings the coach of the Pirates was questioned about failure to teach the players how to warn about possible dangers—not a failure to warn the players, but the failure to teach players how to give a warning. It was also alleged that having the word Nutrilite on the back of the Pirates uniforms was a great benefit by way of advertising. The appellate court addressed the issue of corporate sponsorship by adding: "it would be unsafe for corporations to make charitable contributions if they were held accountable for the actions of the recipients" (*Mann v. Nutrilite*, 1955). In today's legal climate, Bessie Baker would also be named as a defendant, and the four corporations would probably settle out of court in order to avoid negative publicity. Corporate sponsors are critical to many Youth Sport programs, and to hold these sponsors liable for the actions of team members would eliminate a source of funding necessary for Youth Sport.

Berrum v. Powalisz: Negligent Maintenance

Rose Powalisz went to a Little League game and sat in the bleachers behind a fence that was damaged and worn with holes (*Berrum v. Powalisz*, 1957). Two eleven-year-old Little League players found a broken bat, put it back together, and were swinging the bat when it broke apart and flew through the hole in the screen and hit Rose. Powalisz sued the Berrum Little League claiming that the maintenance of the screen behind home plate was negligent conduct. The Little League claimed that Powalisz, as an adult, saw the holes in the screen but chose to sit there anyway, and assumed the risk of injury. The Little League also claimed that the accident was so unusual that they could not have anticipated that injury. The trial court held:

> an invitee who paid for the privilege of using the facilities is not required to examine the safety of the facility. There is an assumption that the facility is safe, and an invitee is not contributory negligent for failing to check the screen and grandstands (*Berrum v. Powalisz*, 1957).

The trial court added:

> the hazard was reasonable and one that could be anticipated and thus the operators of the ball park were responsible for protecting the spectators. Assumption of risk requires actual knowledge of a hazard or it can not be said that the risk was assumed (*Berrum v. Powalisz*, 1957).

Owners and operators of sports facilities owe a duty to protect spectators. If there had been no hole in the screen, the injury to Powalisz could have been prevented. The Supreme Court of Nevada held: "the owners and operators of a facility are responsible for providing a safe environment, not the spectators" (*Berrum v. Powalisz*, 1957). When spectators go to a game or event they should not have to worry about being injured.

Stafford v. Catholic Youth Organization: Duty to Protect Spectators

Emory Stafford, age 12, was watching a wrestling match at the Catholic Youth Organization (CYO) when he was injured (*Stafford v. Catholic Youth Organization*, 1967). While he was sitting on the edge of the mat, Stafford's leg became entangled with one of the wrestlers and he suffered "an oblique fracture of the upper portion of the fibula and a spiral fracture of the lower portion of the tibia". The trial court awarded the young man damages in the amount of $3,000 and the defendants appealed. The trial court judge held: "Stafford was a spectator and not a participant and the assumption of risk doctrine did not apply" (*Stafford v. Catholic Youth Organization*, 1967). The Louisiana Court of Appeals reversed the district court ruling and dismissed the plaintiff's suit. The court of appeals could find no example of negligence or negligent conduct on the part of the participant or supervisor and found that the defendants were not liable for damages. The Court of Appeals of Louisiana held: "Stafford was unfortunately injured, but the injury was an accident and not the result of negligence" (*Stafford v. Catholic Youth Organization*, 1967). Not every injury is the result of negligence, but unfortunately it takes a court of law to determine what is negligence. Would the CYO have been better off moving all spectators and non-participants away from the wrestling mats and the competition? Yes, crowd control and crowd safety is a big part of the responsibility of organizations that invite the public to sporting events. Did anybody win in this case? No, the CYO was found to be not liable, but they had to pay expensive legal fees, and Emory Stafford still had a broken leg.

Inadequate Facilities

Kozera v. Town of Hamburg

Stanley Kozera was attending a Little League baseball game when he was hit in the eye during pregame batting practice (*Kozera v. Town of Hamburg*, 1972). Kozera sued the Town of Hamburg claiming that the town was negligent in constructing, operating, and maintaining the baseball diamond. The plaintiff claimed that the facilities and equipment were inadequate to protect spectators and that supervision was not sufficient during the game. Kozera was sitting in the third base dugout watching the coach fill out the line up card when he was hit in the right eye. There was a screened area behind home plate where plaintiff could have watched batting practice, and there was no evidence of any structural defects in the facility and no factional evidence of a lack of supervision. The Supreme Court, Appellate Division of New York held: "a spectator assumes the risk necessarily incident to baseball as long as those risks are not unduly enhanced by the negligence of the owner of the ball park" (*Kozera v. Town of Hamburg*, 1972). The complaint was dismissed. Kozera assumed the risk of injury because he was in the dugout area, when there was a safe area where the spectators could watch the game. If Kozera had not been in the dugout, the injury would have been prevented, a good reason to keep spectators out of harms way and in the bleachers where they need to be. Just as too many cooks spoil the stew, too many spectators in the playing area create too many risks for themselves and the participants. Dennis Rodman became embroiled in controversy during the 1997 National Basketball Association (NBA) season when he kicked a photographer. Kicking the photographer was an unacceptable act, and not to excuse Rodman, but the photographer was lying on the floor close to the playing court, putting himself and the players at risk. What if Rodman had tripped over the photographer and had blown out a knee, ending a career? Do we need photographers and spectators that close to the playing field? Athletic administrators and officials have to protect the health and safety of participants and spectators which is not an easy task with spectators wanting to get close to the action. Since spectators and fans do not always act in their own best interest, it is the responsibility of the League, or organization to protect the spectators if at all possible.

Jackson v. Cartwright School District

The Cartwright Little League was involved in a lawsuit when Iva Jackson slipped on a ramp while leaving a game where her son was playing (*Jackson v. Cartwright School District*, 1980). The Little League field was owned and operated by the local school district and the playground was open for general use by the public before and after the league games. Jackson and her husband had used the ramp 12 times and had complained to Anthony Mussi, Safety Director for the Cartwright Little League about the condition of the ramp. The Jacksons never complained to the school district and there had been no other complaints to either the Little League or School District. On the day of the accident there were two other gates open and available for use by the spectators and participants. The superior court judge held: "Plaintiff is precluded from recovery since she was aware that the ramp had been slippery in the past and yet continued to use that ramp" (*Jackson v. Cartwright School District*, 1980). The superior court ruled that since Little League did not have possession or control of the facility, it was the school board that was responsible for maintenance and upkeep of the facility and not Little League. One important factor was that there were alternative exits that Iva Jackson could have used to enter and leave the ball park. Also, if the school board had been notified of the problem and chose not to make the corrections needed, the case might have been decided differently. Several years ago there was a similar situation in Augusta County, Virginia, when a parent slipped while leaving a Little League football game and was injured. The stadium had been inspected, was well maintained, and there was no evidence of negligence on the part of the League or the school district. However, the school district and its insurance carrier elected to pay the medical expenses of the injured parent instead of being sued and going to court. The school district, their attorney, and the insurance carrier all believed that to settle the claim as quickly as possible, without the adverse publicity of a lawsuit was the best alternative. However, what that does is drive up the cost of insurance premiums, which are paid with tax dollars, so the public really pays, and there is less money going to instruction.

Bleachers

One area where there has been litigation on the high school and college level is when spectators have been injured when bleachers have collapsed. In *Taylor v. Hardee* (1958) spectators sought recovery for injuries when a bleacher negligently constructed collapsed. Plaintiff spectator brought action against the city and school district in *Novak v. City of Delavan* (1966) for injuries when bleachers collapsed at an athletic event. *Witherspoon v. Haft* (1952) involved a lawsuit over temporary bleachers that were not fastened properly. In the case of *Parker v. Warren* a spectator sued the promoter when bleachers collapsed during a wrestling match. In *Woodring v. Board of Education of Manhasset* (1981) a wrongful death suit was brought against the School District when a platform railing collapsed. Plaintiff was awarded $1,400,000 in damages and the appeals court found evidence that:

1. School District lacked a preventive maintenance program.
2. The platform was improperly constructed.
3. The gymnasium was not inspected on a regular basis.
4. The platform was used extensively, and the injury was foreseeable if the railings were not properly maintained and constructed (Wong, 1994).

These cases demonstrate that construction, maintenance, and inspections of the bleachers are critical for spectator safety. Even though most cases are on the high school and college level, if history has taught us anything, it is that we will have cases in the future on the Youth Sport level. Glenn Wong, in his book *Essentials of Amateur Sports Law*, maintains that facility owners and operators have three areas of concern in providing a safe facility:

1. Duty to protect spectators from injurious and defective products.
2. Duty to maintain the facility and equipment in the facility.
3. Duty to protect spectators from harm caused by other spectators (Wong, 1994).

Ronald Kaiser in his book *Liability and Law in Recreation, Parks and Sports* addresses the issue of bleachers when he states that facility operators have been held liable for injuries when seating structures collapsed, when seats were not properly attached to the floor, when rotten wood was used in construction and when needed repairs were not undertaken (Kaiser, 1986). Kaiser emphasizes that there needs to be a periodical inspection of the seating facilities to ensure safe occupancy (see Appendix H). Walter Champion in *Sports Law* states that facility operators have a duty to maintain premises in a reasonably safe condition, and to supervise the conduct of spectators so as to prevent injury (Champion, 1993).

We want spectators at sporting events because they add to the excitement of the contest and offer support to the participants. However, these cases demonstrate that Youth Sport coaches and administrators have an obligation to provide a safe as possible environment for the spectators to observe the action. We have to see spectators as part of the complete and total package, part of the event itself, and if we want to avoid litigation, we have to protect the spectator just like the participants.

Guidelines for the Protection of Spectators

In summary, there are several guidelines for the Youth Sport administrator to follow in order to help protect spectators:

1. Develop a preventive maintenance program by inspecting all facilities and equipment on a regular basis.
2. Provide adequate security. Security can be delegated out to local law enforcement agencies or handled in house.

3. Remove spectators from the playing areas if at all possible.
4. Supervise spectators as well as participants.
5. Warn spectators about possible dangers such as foul balls in baseball and errant pucks in hockey.
6. Maintain all protective screens and equipment.
7. Provide first aid and emergency medical treatment for all spectators.
8. Make sure all entrance and exit ramps are safe and debris free.

After the Facts

Nine-year-old Johnny Lupoli of Wallingford, Connecticut, knows that his goal of both pitching for the New York Yankees and playing linebacker for the New York Giants is a long shot. But he has ruled out at least one career alternative. "He doesn't want to be a lawyer," says his mother, Susan. On May 6, 1995, Johnny, a pitcher for Kovacs Insurance in the Yalesville Little League, overthrew his catcher during a pregame warmup session and hit a spectator. Now he finds himself the sole defendant in a $15,000 lawsuit.

The suit was filed two weeks before Christmas by Carol LaRosa, who was hit by the toss and is seeking damages, and by LaRosa's husband, Thomas, who is suing for "a loss of consortium." The

LaRosas' attorney, Joseph DeLucia, says that Carol received 60 stitches and has a one-inch scar on her jaw. But the question remains as to why the LaRosas, whose son was one of Johnny's teammates, did not seek relief from the league's insurance carrier, or, if they felt compelled to sue, why adults, such as coaches, were not named instead of a nine-year-old boy.

"Lawsuits are a search for the truth," says DeLucia. "At the time the suit was brought, all the facts were not known. As they become known, it's possible that other defendants will be brought in." Such as Little League Baseball? "That's a possibility, DeLucia confirms. But isn't there an implied risk for the spectators? "In Connecticut there is the doctrine of the assumption of risk," DeLucia explains in perfect legalese. "There was no game going on. It was a warmup session. Does a nine-year-old boy know that it's dangerous to throw near a crowd? I know when I was nine I had a rifle arm."

With thousands of nine-year-old rifle-arms throwing thousands of baseballs as thousands of Little League parents look on, the likelihood of an errant throw is obvious. It's sad, but emblematic of our times, that such an incident results in litigation (*Sports Illustrated*, 1996).

References

Bango v. Carteret Lions Club, 49 A 2d. 57 (New Jersey, 1951).

Berrum v. Powalisz, 317 P. 2d. 1090 (Nevada, 1957).

Carol LaRosa et al. v. John Lapoli, 15829 (Connecticut, 1997).

Champion, Walter T. *Sports Law.* West Publishing Company, St. Paul, Minnesota, 1993.

Christianson v. Hager et al., 64 N.W. 2d. 35 (Minnesota, 1954).

Dougherty, Neil J., David Auxter, Alan S. Goldberger and Gregg S. Heinzmann. *Sport, Physical Education and the Law.* Human Kinetics Publishers, Champaign, Illinois, 1994.

Jackson v. Cartwright School District and Cartwright Little League Inc., 607 P. 2d. 975 (Arizona, 1980).

Kaiser, Ronald A. *Liability and Law in Recreation, Parks and Sports.* Prentice-Hall, Englewood Cliffs, New Jersey, 1986.

Kozera v. Town of Hamburg, 337 N. 45 2d. 761 (New York, 1972).

Mann v. Nutrilite, Inc., 289 P. 2d. 282 (California, 1955).

Murphy v. Jarvis Chevrolet Company, 34 N.E. 2d. 310 (Illinois, 1941).

Novak v. City of Delavan, 143 N.W. 2nd. 6 (Wisconsin, 1966).

Parker v. Warren, 503 S.W. 2nd. 938 (Tennessee, 1973).

Stafford v. Catholic Youth Organization, 202 So. 2d. 333 (Louisiana, 1967).

Swanson, Richard and Betty Spears. *History of Sport and Physical Education in the United States*. Brown and Benchmark, Madison, Wisconsin, 1995.

Taylor v. Hardee, 102 S.E. 2nd 218 (South Carolina, 1958).

"The Windup, the Pitch, the Suit," *Sports Illustrated*, January 15, 1996.

Watford v. Evening Star Newspaper Co., 211 F. 2d. 31 (Washington D.C., 1954).

Witherspoon v. Hart, 106 N.E. 2nd 296 (Ohio, 1952).

Wong, Stacy. "Ballplayer Loses Round in Court," *The Hartford Courant*, February 7, 1997.

Woodring v. Board of Education of Manhasset, 435 N.Y.S. 2nd. 52 (New York, 1981).

Chapter 6

Coaches in Youth Sport

No man is too good to be the athletic coach for youth.
Amos Alonzo Stagg

Coaching Challenges

Today, coaches in Youth Sport face the greatest challenges ever. Volunteer coaches are being held to a higher standard of care now more than ever because of the importance placed on sport by adults. The Youth Sport coach is expected to be Vince Lombardi, Dean Smith, Tom Lasorda, and Phil Jackson all rolled up into one. Vince Lombardi never coached children, he coached men and he was paid very well to be successful. Today's Youth Sport coach is usually an unpaid volunteer, and 85% of the time is also the parent of one of the players (Dash, 1996). Sometimes the parent may never have played the sport that he or she is coaching, but volunteered to try so that there would be a team. These coaches have the best of intentions, but we expect more than good intentions from our coaches today. Unfortunately, coaches may find themselves in a court of law as a defendant in a lawsuit. A Little League coach in Anderson, South Carolina is suing a rival coach and the city for being viciously beaten after a Little League game in 1996 (*Charlotte Observer*, 1997). In 1995 a Little League coach in Kernersville, North Carolina was arrested and charged with molesting a player (Kunar, 1995). The local Little League voted to allow the coach to continue coaching his team while the investigation continued. Officials for the Forsyth County District Attorney's office dropped the felony charges when there was not enough physical evidence to try the case. In June of 1995, in the first inning of a Pony League game in Asheboro, North Carolina, between the Rotary Club and the Sportswerks, one of the coaches hollered at his pitcher to pop somebody, get their butts off of the plate. In the third inning of the game, the pitcher hit an opposing batter on the leg (Griffin, 1995).

Assault

The Pony League Coach was arrested and charged with simple assault for telling his pitcher to back the batters off of the plate. The coach was put on probation by the city and suspended for a game. Parent William Mc-Swaim in the summer of 1991 attacked his son's Youth Baseball coach with a tire iron and a gun, according to court testimony. McSwaim was angry over his nine-year-old son's lack of playing time and called Coach Blake Connor to discuss the situation. During the meeting between parent and coach, a fight started and William McSwaim was killed (Griffin, 1995). In the murder trial that followed, Coach Connor was found not guilty of voluntary manslaughter. One coach gets attacked by another coach, one coach is arrested for assault, while another stands accused of sexual abuse, and a parent is killed when a discussion became a heated argument. Being a volunteer coach of a Youth Sports team is not easy. A Youth Sport coach is expected to provide a healthy atmosphere, expert instruction, manage risks, relate to children and adults, have fun, keep everybody happy, and win championships. An impossible task for a paid professional, much less an untrained volunteer. In addition to being called names, becoming unpopular, and being assaulted, Youth Sport coaches today have to worry about being held liable for damages when a player is injured. When a player is injured, no matter how minor or how serious, the volunteer coach may find himself as a defendant in a law suit.

Little League Liability Law

In Chapter Four we discussed the Joey Fort case where two volunteer Little League coaches were sued for damages when a ten-year-old lost a ball in the sun and was hit in the eye. The two coaches were sued for $750,000, but settled out of court for $25,000. Youth Sport coaches became very scarce in New Jersey after the Fort case was settled. The lack of coaches became so pronounced that the State of New Jersey stepped in to solve the problem. In 1986 the New Jersey Legislature passed a law to protect volunteer coaches from litigation and liability. The 1986 "Little League Liability Law" was an effort to protect volunteers from tort liability and also to require leagues to establish safety orientation and training programs for coaches (Byrne, 1989). The first test case to the New Jersey legislation came one day after the law went into effect on May 12, 1986. The case of *Byrne v. Boys Baseball League* involved an 11-year-old player George C. Byrne, and Coach Dennis Bonk. George Byrne was enrolled in the Fords Clara Barton Baseball League, Inc., a league, although not affiliated with Little League Baseball, was organized and structured

very much the same. Coach Dennis Bonk told Byrne to go warm up the pitcher, and during warm ups Byrne was struck in the eye by a pitched ball. Byrne was wearing most of the catcher's protective equipment, but not a catcher's mask, a violation of League rules. The parents sued Coach Bonk for damages alleging both ordinary negligence and willful, wanton, reckless conduct, and gross negligence. Bonk filed for summary judgment dismissing the complaint against him based on immunity granted under the Little League Liability Act. The 1986 legislative act stated in paragraph C, that:

> nothing in this section shall be deemed to grant immunity to any person causing damage by his willful, wanton, or grossly negligent act of commission or omission, nor to any coach, manager or official who has not participated in a safety program established by the league or team which he is affiliated (Byrne, 1989).

Safety Program Participation

The defendant never claimed to have participated in a safety program, because the League failed to provide one for him. However, Bonk still believed that he was entitled to immunity from liability because of the New Jersey Little League Act. It was then left up to the State Courts to determine legislative intent. The trial court declined to read the Statute as requiring the establishment of a safety and training program for volunteers, and since there was no league safety program for the defendant to attend, Bonk was entitled to statutory immunity. The Superior Court of New Jersey ruled that prior training was at the heart of the immunity concept in the Little League Liability Law and that a volunteer who had not participated in a prescribed safety program is barred from reliance on statutory immunity. The superior court dismissed the summary judgment in favor of Dennis Bonk and remanded the case back to the trial court. With or without participation in a safety program, the 1986 and the 1988 amended version of the Little League Act did not protect any person causing willful, wanton, or grossly negligent acts of commission or omission. No matter what a state legislature does to protect volunteer coaches, courts are reluctant to allow negligence. Negligence has always been determined in civil court and legislative attempts to override common law tradition will be unsuccessful in all probability. To give a class of citizens, such as coaches, blanket protection, to excuse a negligent act before the act has been committed, and to not allow an injured victim any recourse for an injury has never been the American way. If a child is injured as the result of negligence, that child deserves the opportunity to receive compensation. I do not believe allowing coaches to be negligent in their actions because they are volunteers will pass judicial review. Coaches should not rely on state legislatures to protect them from lawsuits. Volunteer coaches need to protect themselves, and that is accomplished through education and training.

What Can the Coach Do?

What is the Youth Sport coach to do? What does the volunteer/parent need to know? According to Lynne Gaskin, Professor of Physical Education and Recreation at The State University of West Georgia, the Youth Sport coach needs to establish rules and regulations for the particular sport, communicate to the participants what the rules are, and then enforce the rules and regulations (Gaskin, 1993). Gaskin believes that failure to establish rules and then failure by the coach to implement the rules may constitute negligence. If the league or organization has established particular rules then the coach needs to communicate and enforce those rules to team members. In the earlier cited case of *Byrne v. Boys Baseball League* if Coach Bonk had been enforcing the league rule that catchers, even when warming up a pitcher, wear a mask, then the injury to George C. Byrne Jr. would in all probability have been prevented and there would have been no need for litigation. Gaskin believes that rules are important. Albert

Figone, Associate Professor in Health and Physical Education at Humboldt State University, adds that coaches need to plan their activities very carefully (Figone, 1989). We have read stories about the professional coach that sleeps in his office all week working on the big "game plan" and college and high school coaches who have every minute of every practice planned out and scheduled. Some coaches may go to the extreme, but planning is important, and planning can help reduce the risk of injury. A well-planned, thought out and structured practice should be a safer practice. The better prepared a coach is, the less room is left for chance and bad luck. Figone also believes that one of the major legal duties of a coach is to warn participants about the potential dangers involved in an activity. Warnings should be clear, and sensible, but not intimidating or scary. Exactly how a coach is to put the fear of God into young participants, without putting the fear of sport into them has not been determined. All we know is that the younger the child, the less experienced the child, the more important the warnings become. The parents also need to understand what risks their children will be taking by playing a sport. Parents know what the risks of letting a teenager drive a car, and they still let them drive, but they know up front that there are risks. There is a hotel chain that, as part of its marketing campaign, acknowledges that Americans do not like surprises. Coaches need to understand that philosophy and plan their practices and warn their players about possible dangers of participating in sport. It has been recommended that coaches video tape the first practice or meeting where rules, regulations, and warnings are reviewed. A video tape can be evidence of what was said in the meeting, and who attended the meeting.

Specific Supervision

Another guideline for Youth Sport coaches comes from Herb Appenzeller in his book *Athletics and the Law* (Appenzeller, 1975). Appenzeller emphasizes that coaches supervise games and practices very carefully. Specific supervision, according to Appenzeller, is the close supervision of athletes performing a sport activity. Specific supervision is what a coach does, it requires the coach to be at practice and games, to supervise dangerous activities more closely than less dangerous sports. The Youth Sport coach is expected to pay attention, to observe what is going on and to anticipate problems or dangers. According to Paul Proehl:

> Broadly speaking, what is reasonable and what is foreseeable are the criteria for supervising young people. The standard is ordinary prudence, the impossible will not be required, but is often expected (Appenzeller, 1975).

Remember that one of the most frequent causes of litigation is the alleged lack of proper supervision. The Youth Sport coach has to always be careful when calling practice to make sure that an adult is present to help supervise. When children are left on their own, they sometimes get careless and injuries and accidents result. An idle mind may be the devil's workshop according to an old musical, but unsupervised children is a lawsuit waiting to happen. Neighborhood children getting together for a pick up game is entirely different that an organized practice. A scheduled practice creates a duty of care owed by the coach to the players, a legal obligation that can not and should not be dismissed lightly. Parents who encourage their children to participate in Youth Sport expect adult supervision from coaches. Traditionally it has been adult supervision that has made Youth Sport so popular with parents. The parents expectation is that when they drop their son or daughter off at practice, there will be a coach present. It has nothing to do with how much or how little the coach is being paid. No matter how gifted or awkward the player, how minor or serious the injury, that player is still somebody's child.

Teach Proper Technique

The Youth Sport coach not only has to be able to supervise practice and games, but the coach has to be able to teach members of the team correct techniques and skills. The *Fort* case which was settled out of court, raised the issue that coaches have to be able to properly instruct and teach correct techniques. Teaching players in football to lead with their heads, or not showing a baseball player how to slide, are two examples of improper coaching. New rules and techniques have made sport safer to play, and coaches have to stay current with the newest developments. We do not wear leather helmets in football anymore, and we do not run over catchers in baseball are two examples of changes that have been made for safety.

Put the Child's Welfare First

The last guideline for the Youth Sport coach to remember may be the easiest and yet the hardest at the same time. Coaches have to remember to always put the welfare of the child first. Common sense, yes, but in the excitement of competition, playing for the championship, and all the glory, putting the welfare of the child first is sometimes easier said than done. Putting the welfare of the child first, may mean that the star pitcher is not forced to throw with a tired arm, or the key soccer player sits out a game with shin splints. Putting the welfare of the child first may also mean that coaches do not ridicule or embarrass players. According to Bonnie Hutchins, Program Director for the Wisconsin Committee for Prevention of Child

Abuse: "Ridiculing kids and embarrassing them in front of their peers and parents is child abuse" (Dash, 1996). Putting the welfare of the participant first is not hollering and yelling at, or making fun of, players. There is no place in Youth Sport for the coach who is trying to use the success of children to build his own self ego. The "win at all cost" mentality is not appropriate on the youth sport level. According to an old television commercial, a mind is a terrible thing to waste, but the self-image and self-esteem of a child is a terrible thing to destroy. Sports Psychology expert Rick Wolff has developed ten warning signs of a poor coach:

1. The coach physically or verbally abuses athletes.
2. Players themselves are criticized, rather than the behavior.
3. The coach uses profanity.
4. Coach will not listen to suggestions or complaints from parents.
5. Winning is emphasized as the only goal.
6. The coach constantly argues with referees and officials.
7. Cheating is condoned.
8. Coach will not allow all members of the team to play, especially less skillful players.
9. Kids are degraded for losing and praised only for winning.
10. The coach feels personally let down when the team does not measure up to his/her expectations (Dash, 1996).

It is human nature to want to win, to be successful, but the welfare of the players has to be the first priority. Years ago I heard someone remark that a well-officiated contest meant that you did not notice the officials. In Youth Sport a well played game means that you never notice the coaches. Youth Sport is not about coaches, it is about players. The Youth Sport coach sets the tone, sets the example, and it needs to be positive in every way.

The competition, glory, honor, and rewards of sport have always been for adults, men and now more recently women. Today we are providing the same experiences of competition, glory, honor, and rewards for children and it makes the job of coach very difficult. Coaching children can be very frustrating and at the same time very rewarding, and it is in the very least demanding. Coaching Youth Sports today is an awesome responsibility, because the coach is on the front line, he is responsible for the health, safety, and welfare of the participants.

Guidelines for Coaches

In my opinion, there are six basic guidelines for the Youth Sport coach to remember:

1. Explain, demonstrate, communicate, and enforce rules.

2. Always supervise practice and games.
3. Warn participants and parents about the risks and dangers of the activity.
4. Teach proper and correct techniques and skills.
5. Plan, always prepare for practice and games.
6. Put the welfare of the child first.

Coaches have an awesome responsibility and obligation to the children and it is something that should not be taken lightly.

After the Facts

"He loved coaching and sports cars," his wife said, "but he really loved coaching."

Danny William Hopper, who never berated a player in front of others, died June 10 at Presbyterian Hospital on his 14th wedding anniversary. He was 52 and had coached sports for Steele Creek Athletic Association for more than 10 years.

His memorial service at Durham Memorial Baptist Church drew about 500 mourners. "People spilled out in the yard," said Scotty Jackson, a player's mother. "Young men—baseball players he'd

coached—stood up and gave positive information. It was the most moving experience I ever had. He made a difference in their lives."

Her son, Matt, had played on one of Hopper's teams. "He never berated a player in front of anyone," she said. "He would pull him aside, get on his knees, and look him in the face. Then he'd explain the error, pat him on the back and encourage him."

Danny Hopper had coached his own sons, Toby, 23, Colbey, 20, and Joey, almost 11. "He thought the most important thing was being a role model for children," said Hopper's wife, Cindy.

She added, "He wanted to win, but it was not the most important thing. He believed in a fair game and if something happened that was not fair, he was real quick to question it, but not to fuss. He looked for the best in them."

That sense of fairness was a part of Danny Hopper's life. "His jokes were always good-spirited, not at someone's expense," said friend Doni-Raye Kendrick. They'd known each other for 42 years, since both were 10. "From bicycles to bedside..." Kendrick said, "a lifetime of things you can't bring together in a few words. Danny was one of those best friends that only come by once in a lifetime."

Grayland Lowry was another friend who was also a co-worker at Hoechst Celanese, where Hopper, a training coordinator, had worked since 1965. "He was somewhat low key but very innovative," Lowry said. "He brought out the best in people overall, especially their ideas. He never, ever said, 'That was a dumb idea.' He looked for the good."

"He was very dedicated to his job," Cindy Hopper said. "He loved his family and was also dedicated to his church. When he made a commitment, you could count on him to follow through."

He was a member of Durham Memorial Baptist Church for 40 years, served on the finance committee, was associate treasurer, an ordained deacon and a member of the chancel choir and sand in the Lighthouse Quartet.

A tribute by Matt Jackson's father, Sonny, read: "Dan Hopper's a friend, he'll be sorely missed; but we'll see him again...when we make heaven's All Star List."

"He was the same way in life as he was with those boys: kind, caring, very honest and very fair," his wife said. "He was the very epitome of a good Christian."

She added, "I told the hospice lady, 'You never had a chance to know my husband, but he is just a good guy through and through. It leaks out'" (Hostetler, 1997).

References

Appenzeller, Herb. *Athletics and the Law*. The Michie Company, Charlottesville, Virginia, 1975.

Byrne v. Boys Baseball League, 564 A. 2d. 1222 (New Jersey, 1989).

"Coach Reports Attack...Sues," *The Charlotte Observer*, February 23, 1997.

Dash, Julie. "Is Your Child a Tyrant?" *Family Circle*, April 23, 1996.

Dash, Julie. "Unsportsmanlike Behavior," *Family Cicrle*, April 23, 1996.

Figone, Albert J. "Seven Major Legal Duties of a Coach," *Journal of Physical Education, Recreation, and Dance*, September 1989.

Gaskin, Lynne P. "Establishing, Communicating, and Enforcing Rules and Regulations," *Journal of Physical Education, Recreation, and Dance*. February 1993.

Griffin, Anna. "Can Adults Zeal, Steal Youth Baseball's Fun?" *The Charlotte Observer*, July 2, 1995.

Hostetler, Gerry. "Steele Creek Coach was a Role Model for Players," *The Charlotte Observer*, June 20, 1997.

Kunar, Anita. "Coach Back after Charge is Dropped," *Greensboro News and Record*, August 22, 1995.

Underwood, John. "A Century of Honesty," *Sports Illustrated*, 1962.

Chapter 7

Facilities

If America is the real religion of Americans, then the sports arena is our true church.

Norman Mailer

The Little League baseball diamond, the Pop Warner football field, a city soccer complex, are special places for children. Michael Novak, writing in his book the *Joy of Sports*, states: "Arenas are like monasteries; individual games imprint on memory single images blazing as if from an illuminated text. Awesome places, a familiar, quiet sort of awe. Our Cathedrals" (Novak, 1976). Digging cleats into the turf, grass stains on uniforms, bleachers all are part of the sporting experience for most people. The mowed grass, the freshly raked infield, the painted lines or the smell of a locker room all create memories for participants in sport. Unfortunately, it is those same arenas, those "cathedrals" that also cause injuries. One of the leading claims in lawsuits involving injuries in sport is unsafe facilities. How do we protect participants and spectators from unsafe facilities? How do we make all facilities safe? As the numbers of participants and spectators increase in Youth Sport, so does opportunity for more injuries increase. This chapter will examine several lawsuits to determine what are some problem areas, and then develop a set of guidelines for safer facilities.

Problem Areas

One of the sports hardest hit by injuries related to facility problems has been soccer. According to the United States Consumer Product Safety Commission (CPSC) there have been at least 27 deaths since 1979 attributed to movable soccer goals (JAMA, 1994). A 16-year-old boy and two friends climbed on a mobile soccer goal post at a high school soccer field, with the result that the 16-year-old was struck in the head by the goal (JAMA, 1994). The youth died one hour later from severe blunt head trauma with multiple head fractures and cerebral edema. In another case, a father and brother lifted a corner goal post to remove the net, but the goal post fell over striking and killing the three-year-old son. A nine-year-old boy was playing goalie during a team practice when a gust of wind blew over the unstaked steel soccer goal post and fractured the goalie's femur (JAMA, 1987). The goal post had been moved before practice and the steel stakes that secure it to the ground had been left behind. As a result, a nine-year-old boy spent six weeks in the hospital and four months being disabled before regaining use of his leg. These are just a few examples of injuries caused by soccer goals, goals that can make any facility hazardous. In 1989, eight-year-old Nicholas Marcotte died when a soccer goal on a school playground tipped over and struck him on the head (Berg, 1994). Nicholas' parents Robert and Jyme Marcotte sued the school district, Process Engineering (the local firm that manufactured the goal post), and the Timberlane Youth Soccer League that installed the goal. A jury awarded the parents $925,000 from the three defendants. How many recreation departments and youth leagues realize how dangerous unsecured and movable soccer goal posts are? The Consumer Product Safety Commission with a coalition of soccer goal manufacturers, has issued a set of safety guidelines for using goal posts. The guidelines are:

1. Anchor or counterweight portable goals.
2. Remove nets when goals are not in use.
3. Disassemble and store goals at end of season.
4. Place safety labels on goals (Berg, 1994).

A soccer goal seems harmless enough, but these examples demonstrate that safety can not always be taken for granted. Unless someone gets hurt, many administrators and coaches do not see the danger, until after the accident when it is too late. A year after the initial guidelines for soccer goals were issued, the CPSC added some additional guidelines for the use and storage of soccer goals:

1. Use moveable goals on level fields only.
2. Check for structural integrity before each use and replace missing or damaged parts immediately.
3. Instruct players on the safe handling and dangers of movable goals.
4. Do not allow climbing on the net or goal frame (Berg, 1994).

Soccer is a sport that continues to grow in popularity and more and more goals dot the landscape of schools, playgrounds, and parks. Understanding the risk of movable goal posts is just one aspect of the sport that today's youth coach, referee, and administrator is expected to know.

Susan Reilly was a soccer player who slipped in a mud puddle and injured herself playing on a field that was covered with puddles (*Reilly v. Long Island Junior Soccer League*, 1995). It had rained prior to, and dur-

ing the game on the day that Reilly was injured (Reilly, 1995). The plaintiff sued the soccer league, soccer club, and the soccer referees for damages, but the supreme court, appellate division held that the player voluntarily assumed the risk that she might slip on the playing field. The court ruled:

> the alleged injury producing condition was not concealed, and the player was fully aware of its existence prior to her voluntary participation. Plaintiff had competed in inclement weather before, and had played on the same field on other occasions (*Reilly v. Long Island Junior Soccer League*, 1995).

The court emphasized that the condition of the field was not concealed and that the plaintiff knew the risk involved. Knowledge of dangerous field conditions is important when using the assumption of risk defense against negligence. Would it have been better to have postponed the game, with a wet field, mud puddles, and it still raining? Probably yes. Susan Reilly assumed the risk, but if the Northport/Cow Harbor United Soccer Club and the Long Island Soccer Referee's Association had postponed the game, an injury might have been prevented and also expensive litigation. The supreme court, appellate division, ruled that Reilly voluntarily assumed the risk, but how many athletes or players will refuse to take the field if their team is playing?

Environmental Factors

In sports, and especially in Youth Sport, leaders need to use common sense and good judgment when deciding whether to play or not. This could mean stopping, delaying, or postponing games or practices for any number of reasons. When a facility is a field or stadium, weather becomes part of that facility. What are the guidelines for heat, cold, and lightning? Environmental stress can have a very negative effect on an athlete and can pose a serious health threat. Some environmental factors that can be of major concern to coaches, administrators, and officials are hyperthermia, hypothermia, and electrical storms. According to Daniel Arnheim and William Prentice in *Principles of Athletic Training*, the prevention of hyperthermia involves:

1. gradual acclimatization of the athlete,
2. identification of susceptible individuals,
3. lightweight uniforms,
4. routine weight record keeping,
5. unrestricted fluid replacement,
6. well-balanced diet,
7. routine temperature and humidity readings.

When there is heat, humidity, and bright sunshine, the Youth Sport coach needs to take extra precautions. Basic guidelines for heat:

1. 82–85° coach should be alert to problems with athletes.
2. 85–88° practice for athletes unacclimated to heat should be curtailed.
3. 88–90° practice should be curtailed for everybody.
4. over 90° all practice is stopped—skill sessions, demonstrations, etc. (Arnheim, 1997).

Basic guidelines for dealing with heat and humidity:

1. 80–90°, humidity under 70%—watch athletes who are overweight.
2. 80–90°, humidity over 70%—give players 10 minute rest every hour, change tee shirts when wet, constant and careful supervision of athletes is needed.
3. 90–100°, humidity over 70%—practice should be suspended, or a shortened program without equipment could be used (Arnheim, 1997).

Eight steps to prevent heat injury:

1. Have a good physical exam and a complete medical history on each participant;

2. Evaluate the pre-practice condition of the athletes;
3. Measure temperature and humidity at practice;
4. Acclimatize athletes to heat gradually;
5. Monitor body weight loss during practice;
6. Monitor clothing and uniforms;
7. Provide water and rest periods regularly, usually every 20 minutes;
8. Know the trouble signs:
   a. headache,
   b. nausea,
   c. mental slowness,
   d. cramps,
   e. incoherence,
   f. weakness,
   g. faintness (Arnheim, 1997).

Hypothermia

Every year we read about the tragic death of athletes who suffer heat stroke during practice in the summer months. Hypothermia, or injuries associated with low temperatures can also pose a threat to the health of athletes. The combination of cold, wind, and dampness creates an environment where the athlete is susceptible to hypothermia. If an athlete fails to warm up properly, becomes inactive for an extended period of time, or is exposed to excessive dampness or wetness, the athlete may suffer a cold-related injury. There are several steps to take to prevent hypothermia:

1. Clothes for participants should be geared to the weather.
2. Clothing should not restrict movement, and be as lightweight as possible.
3. Athletes should dress in thin layers of clothing that can be easily added or removed.
4. Before exercising, during breaks, or rest periods, warm-up suits should be worn to prevent chilling.
5. Special precautions should be taken if the conditions are cold, wet, and windy (Arnheim, 1997).

Electrical Storms (Lightning)

Another environment hazard for sports is the electrical storm. The number two cause of death by weather phenomena every year is lightning, accounting for an average of 110 deaths per year. Lightning is dangerous because it is so unpredictable and often there is little if any warning. The

National Lightning Safety Institute has several guidelines to follow when confronted with an electrical storm:

1. When thunder is heard begin to prepare a defense plan.
2. An indoor facility is the safest place to be.
3. If an indoor facility is not available, a car is next best.
4. Avoid:
   a. water,
   b. metal bleachers,
   c. metal cleats,
   d. umbrellas,
   e. light poles,
   f. golf clubs,
   g. motors,
   h. power tools,
   I. high ground,
   j. golf carts.
5. Do not stand under:
   a. tall trees,
   b. telephone poles,
   c. open-sided rain shelters,
   d. tents,
   e. isolated trees.
6. If lightning is striking nearby:
   a. avoid direct contact with other people;
   b. remove all metal objects from your person;
   c. crouch down, with feet together and hands on knees;
   d. do not lie flat.
7. Allow 30 minutes to pass after the last sound of thunder or lightning strike to resume play or practice (Appenzeller and Baron, 1997).

Wind, rain, heat, cold, and lightning are all part of an outdoor facility, and affect the safety of the facility. We may not be able to predict or control the weather, but coaches, administrators, and officials have to be prepared to handle whatever happens.

Hector Gonzalez sued the City of New York for an injury he sustained sliding into home plate at Prospect Park field (*Gonzalez v. City of New York*, 1994). There was a defect in the playing field surrounding home plate that Gonzalez had observed prior to the accident. The supreme court, appellate division held that the plaintiff assumed the risk inherent in sliding into home plate. The defect was so obvious that to go ahead and play created the assumption of risk defense for the defendant.

The case of *Rubenstein v. Woodstock Riding Club* gives a good explanation of the assumption of risk doctrine. Samara Rubenstein was a

12-year-old participant in the "Fitting and Showmanship" event conducted at the Woodstock Riding Club, Inc. Contestants in the event, while on foot, lead their horse around the ring at a trot, and then would stop their horse behind the other horses in a head to tail formation. Samara had difficulty controlling her horse (Flair) and could not stop him until the horse was directly behind the defendants horse (Winsome). Flair then nudged Winsome in the rear and Winsome kicked, fracturing Samara's right leg. Samara's father commenced negligence action seeking damages and derivative losses for his daughter's injury. As a general rule:

> participants in a sporting event or activity may be held to have consented to those injury-causing events which are known or reasonably foreseeable. An assessment of whether a participant assumed a risk depends on the openness and obviousness of the risks, the participants skill and experience, as well as his or her conduct under the circumstances (*Rubenstein v. Woodstock Riding Club*, 1994).

The defendants argued that in a horse show, horses are strong and sometimes unpredictable animals and there is always an inherent risk of injury. Since Samara had taken lessons for one and a half years, and knew to keep a six to ten foot distance between the horses, the supreme court, appellate division, held that the plaintiff assumed the risk of being injured in the show. If the risk is open and obvious and the participant has the skill and experience, assumption of risk may be the best defense for the defendant.

Ever Alvarez sued the Village of Hampstead when he was injured playing soccer. The Supreme Court, Appellate Division, held that: "plaintiff had played soccer approximately 25 times on the field, voluntarily participated, assumed the risk of running upon uneven terrain of the ballfield." Alvarez was not able to recover damages for his personal injuries because he had assumed the risk of injury when he decided to play. The court held that the dangers were obvious and foreseeable and that plaintiff chose to participate of his own free will (*Alvarez v. Incorporated Village of Hempstead*, 1996).

Failure to Warn

Ten-year-old Edith LeJeune was injured while participating in a tee-ball game on school board property, leased by the Egan Community Recreation Department for use by the Egan Little League (*LeJeune v. Acadia Parish School Board*, 1987). There was a barrier between the parking lot and the baseball field which consisted of a cable suspended through a series of concrete posts. The cable was about as high as Edith's knees and she tripped over it severely injuring her left knee. Edith suffered a broken knee and torn ligaments and her father Roderick LeJeume sued on her behalf claiming that the suspended cable was an unreasonable risk. The trial court found that the cable was visible, the accident occurred in daylight, that grass did not obscure it, and that the cable was not an unreasonable risk The father appealed the trial court's decision and the Court of Appeal of Louisiana affirmed the trial court's ruling. The court of appeals held that the ease at which a dangerous condition can be observed and whether or not the defect would cause injury to a prudent person would be two factors to consider. The plaintiffs were not able to prove that the cable fence presented an unreasonable risk of harm. The defendants were not found negligent, but would it be better to paint the cable a bright shade of orange, to make it more visible to spectators and participants alike. In Youth Sport there is no legal mandate to paint the cable, but a bright paint job would make the cable a safer part of a facility.

Bleacher Safety

In the case of *South Gwinnett Athletic Association, Inc. v. Nash*, a lawsuit was brought against a Community Athletic Association for unsafe facilities. Eight-year-old Adam Nash was injured when a temporary bleacher wall he was attempting to climb collapsed. The cinder-block wall was part of an unfinished set of new bleachers, and Adam climbed the wall to watch his younger brother play in a tee-ball game. Adam was halfway up the wall when it collapsed, injuring his leg. Adam's father sued the Association for failure to guard or warn against a dangerous condition. A jury returned a verdict in favor of the Association, and the Nashs' filed a motion for a new trial. The plaintiffs claimed that the Association acted in a willful and malicious manner by not warning people about the dangers of the bleachers under construction. According to the court of appeals, willful and malicious conduct is:

> A willful failure to guard or warn would require actual knowledge of the owner that its property is being used for recreational purpose; that a condition exists involving an unreasonable risk of death or serious bodily harm; that the condition is not apparent to those using the property; and that not having this knowledge, the owner chooses not to guard or warn in disregard of possible consequences (*South Gwinett v. Nash*, 1996).

In fact the Commissioner of the Association Tee-Ball league testified that prior to the game he did warn people about the unfinished bleachers and asked adults to keep children away. The Court of Appeals of

Georgia held that building bleachers at a baseball field is a reasonable thing to do and that the cement wall standing alone presented no risk or danger. Even though not everybody might have heard the announcement about the bleachers, the Commissioner did make an attempt to warn adults and children. The Commissioner made a good faith effort and therefore the Association was not willful or malicious in its actions.

Objects in Playing Field

Ricardo Hernandez was a softball player injured when he slid into a stake protruding from the ground near home plate. Hernandez brought action against the Chicago Park District for damages claiming willful and wanton conduct against the city (*Hernandez v. Chicago Park District*, 1995). The jury returned a verdict in favor of the softball player and awarded him $192,500 in damages, but the trial court entered a judgment notwithstanding the verdict in favor of the defendant. The plaintiff appealed and the Appellate Court, Cook County ruled against Hernandez. The Softball League had a must slide rule so that no one would get hurt, but when Ricardo obeyed the rule, and slid into home, he caught his left leg on a stake that was above ground. The wooden stake had been placed on the field during construction and had never been removed. Since

no one had seen the stake protruding from the ground in the weeks leading up to the accident, no one had reported it to the Recreation Department, therefore the appellate court held that the Park District may have been negligent, but the conduct was not willful or wanton (*Hernandez v. Chicago Park District*, 1995). However, Justice J. Tully dissented and stated that he would reverse the judgment of the circuit court and he would reinstate the jury's verdict. Tully held that the Park District knew about the stake, used it to line off the field, and therefore the Park District had actually created the danger. Three judges, three votes, a 2-1 decision, one vote switches and Hernandez is awarded $192,500 in damages. It does not take very much to alter or create case law, one vote will do. I have to agree with the dissent in this case, a league rule requiring sliding and a wooden stake left exposed behind home plate creates an inherent risk. If a stake is used to line off base paths, the stake should be buried or covered by foam padding. A big part of facility management is anticipation for preventive action. Objects in the field of play need to be made as safe as possible. Years ago as a high school football coach we traveled to a conference rival for a big game. Before the game an assistant coach took me to the end zone where he showed me a wooden light pole. The light pole, halfway between the goal line and the end zone line was there because the facility was a baseball/football complex. There was no padding on the light pole, no warnings, it was just there. The school did put a pad around the pole the next year, but as far as I know that light pole is still part of the football field. As I said earlier, it might be expensive to move the light pole, but an injury to a participant and a lawsuit.

In Youth Sport cases that we have examined, the majority of decisions favored the defendants and the assumption of risk defense. From tripping over a cable, to collapsing walls, uneven terrain, mud puddles and getting kicked by a horse, plaintiffs were injured. The most serious injuries were the result of the soccer goals that fell over and those decisions favored the plaintiffs. Negligence was alleged in most of the cases, but the conduct was not held to be willful or wanton.

Environmental Principles to Follow

Injuries and lawsuits are both expensive and our goal is to eliminate both if possible. In addition to the guidelines discussed earlier for hyperthermia, hypothermia, and lightning, there are several other environmental principles to follow when making facilities safe:

1. Always begin the day or the practice by inspecting the facility.

2. Check for any hazards or problems that might exist.
3. Make sure that playing surfaces are dry and clear of debris.
4. Make sure walls and goals are padded.
5. Make sure bleachers are in good repair.
6. Make sure that all areas are well lighted, that exits are clearly marked and are not locked.
7. Facilities should be accessible to everyone.
8. Post warning signs and safety rules and regulations for use of the facility.
9. If conditions are questionable for practice or games, postpone or delay the activity until a later time (Appenzeller, 1997).

A Personal Experience

When I was in the first grade, my parents took me to a popular drive in restaurant. After we ordered, my sisters and I got out of the car to run around and play before the food arrived. It was dark and I tripped and landed on a broken bottle, cutting my hand. The food and I made it back to the car at the same time and my parents bandaged my hand with a hamburger wrapper and it was off to the doctor. My hand took 21 stitches and the next day we drove back to the restaurant and my father talked to the manager, about the accident the night before. There was no lawsuit, no lawyers, this was 1958, but the restaurant did stop serving glass bottle drinks and started using paper cups. Another era, another place in time, but the point is that the majority of people still do not want to see others get hurt. We do not want injuries. Even though I should not have been outside running around anyway, the manager agreed that paper cups would be better. There was an accident which caused an injury and a solution was found. Today there would probably be a lawsuit or the threat of a lawsuit, and the safety issue would be addressed by a court of law.

Glenn Wong in his book, *Essentials of Amateur Sports Law* has developed the following guidelines to help facility operators protect themselves against possible litigation. Wong suggests:

1. Anticipate potentially injurious situations in the facility or event site.
2. Ensure that the facility is adequately maintained, perform regular inspections, practice preventive maintenance.
3. Safety should be a top priority by the architects and planning committee when designing a facility.

4. Materials used in the facility should be as safe as possible, examples would be glass, padding, mats, and floors.
5. Designate an individual on the staff or with the organization to serve as the safety expert.
6. Develop a clear written policy concerning safety in the facility, institute procedures for reporting potential problems and document injuries and accidents in detail (Wong, 1994).

Nobody wants to see people get hurt, especially children and nobody wants the injury to be caused by an unsafe facility. We have to monitor facilities very carefully, we have to anticipate problem areas and we have to remember that an ounce of prevention is worth a pound of cure. Be proactive rather than reactive.

After the Facts

The final bell had just rung at Nashoba Regional High School on May 24, 1989. With summer just around the corner, students went running for the outdoors. Some headed to the bus, some to practice, and some to their cars. Joanna Basteri, a sophomore, and Stephen Rausch, a junior, headed for ice cream. However, before

they reached the ice cream parlor their car lost control, flipped on it's side and bent around a tree. Both were killed. They were two of the best soccer players at Nashoba and were extremely popular with their peers. I can remember, as a freshman, hearing the sirens while I was out at track practice. People weren't sure how to handle such a tragedy.

The next day, not even 24 hours later, a group of Joanna and Stephen's closest friends were mourning their loss on the soccer field. The group made a memorial wreath and felt it would be appropriate to hang it from the crossbar. The smallest of the group, Jason Goldfarb, was boosted up onto the crossbar to attach the wreath. After doing so he jumped down. As he did the crossbar came loose, falling and striking Jason on the back of his head. He died later that day in the hospital. The community was devastated (Kendra, 1997).

References

Alvarez v. Incorporated Village of Hempstead, 637 NYS 2d 463 (New York, 1996).

Appenzeller, H. and R. Baron. *From the Gym to the Jury*, Greensboro, North Carolina, vol. 8, no. 5, p. 4, 1997.

Arnheim, Daniel D. And Prentice, William E. *Principles of Athletic Training*. Brown and Benchmark, St. Louis, Missouri, 1997.

Berg, Rick. "Who'll Foot the Bill in Soccer Goal Death?" *Athletic Business*, vol. 18, no. 4, p. 26, April 1994.

Gonzales v. City of New York, 617 NYS 2d. 603 (New York, 1994).

Hendandez v. Chicago Park District, 654 N.E. 2d. 463 (Illinois, 1995).

"Injuries Associated with Soccer Goal Posts," *Jama*, United States, 1979–1993, vol. 271, no. 16, April 27, 1984.

Kendra, Heather. "Soccer Goal Injuries: Absolutely Preventable," *From the Gym to the Jury*, vol. 8, no. 3, 1997.

LeJune v. Acadia Parish School Board, 517 So. 2d. 1030 (Louisiana, 1987).

Novak, Michael. *The Joy of Sports*. Basic Books, Inc., New York, New York, 1976.

Reilly v. Long Island Junior Soccer League, Inc. 216 A.D. 2d 281 (New York, 1995).

Rubenstein v. Woodstock Riding Club, 617 NYS 2d. 603 (New York, 1994).

South Gwinnett Athletic Association, Inc. v. Nash et al., 469 S.E. 2d.
   276 (Georgia, 1996).
Wong, Glenn. *Essentials of Amateur Sports Law.* Second Edition.
   Praeger Publishing, Westport, Connecticut, 1994.

Chapter 8

Gender Issues

Sport participation often enables girls and women to establish identities based on skills respected by peers and the community.
Tini Campbell

Cindy Lowery

In the summer of 1963, I went to stay with my Grandparents on their farm in Marshville, North Carolina and had the opportunity to play Little League Baseball. One Saturday morning we went to play against another team from the nearby town of Wingate. Much to our surprise, the Wingate team had a player who was not a boy, but a girl and she was going to play, against us. Cindy Lowery was a shortstop and pitcher and the first girl to play Little League baseball for the town of Wingate. There were several comments made in the dugout before the game, all in poor taste, but there was nothing we could do to prevent her from playing. It was embarrassing, playing against a girl, but Cindy played well, even striking out several of the Marshville players, and getting a hit. That was 34 years ago on a hot July morning, and I still remember that game, it made an impression on me, and the other young boys from Marshville. For us, Cindy Lowery was a "tomboy" an exception to the way girls were supposed to be, but little did we realize that summer what would happen over the next three decades in sports for women. Cindy thought about going to the next level and playing Babe Ruth Baseball, but she and her family decided not to push the issue. In high school at Forest Hills, Lowery played basketball for four years, because that was the only sport available for girls at that time. Cindy Lowery attended Wingate Junior College after high school where she played basketball, and then transferred to Catawba College in Salisbury, North Carolina and continued her basketball career. While at Catawba, a National Association of Intercollegiate Athletics (NAIA) school she was able to play tennis and softball. Cindy Lowery playing baseball in rural North Carolina was not typical of the role of girls and women in sport in the 1960s. Women who grew up during the 1950s and 1960s were told that vigorous exercise could damage the uterus and cause them to have prob-

lems in childbirth. Women were also warned that playing sports would lead to the development of bulging muscles and other masculine characteristics. Then came Title IX, a law that revolutionized sport participation for women.

Title IX

Section 901 of Title IX of the Education Amendments Act of 1972 states:

> No person in the United States shall on the basis of sex, be excluded from participation in, be denied the benefits of, or be subjected to discrimination under any education program or activity receiving federal financial assistance (Wong, 1994).

Title IX became law on July 1, 1972, as Public Law 92-318, but it only applied to programs, organizations, or agencies that received federal funds. Title IX was an attempt to provide athletic opportunities for women on the high school and college level. Even though Title IX was not about Youth Sport, the legislation did mandate increased sporting opportunities for females on the high school and college level, while at the same time made parents and young women aware of the importance of sport. Title IX rocked the boat, created controversy, and controversy created publicity and publicity created interest. However, the mandate to provide opportunities for women in sport met resistance on the high school, college, and even youth sport level. In 1984, the United States Supreme Court ruled in *Grove City v. Bell* that Title IX did not apply to school athletic programs unless they received federal money. Over 800 cases of alleged discrimination under investigation by the U.S. Department of Education's Office for Civil Rights were dropped after the Grove City decision was handed down. Four years later, Congress passed the Civil Rights Restoration Act which again mandated equal opportunities in athletic competition for women in any organization that received federal money. In 1992, the United States Supreme Court ruled that coaches and athletes could recover financial damages against any school that intentionally violated Title IX (Coakley, 1994). This ruling put gender equity back in the Federal and State Courts, where it has always been in Youth Sport. Women participating in sport has not always been widely accepted, and it has not been just the colleges and high schools, but Youth Sport as well, that have fought the battle over the unlevel playing field. Many Youth Sports organizations have been slow and reluctant to accept female participation. When Youth Leagues fought gender equity, the result has been lawsuits.

A Landmark Case

One of the landmark cases in gender equity and Youth Sport was the *National Organization for Women v. Little League Baseball* (NOW, 1974).

In Hoboken, New Jersey, Maria Pepe was a female pitcher for one of the local Little League teams. When the National Office of Little League, Inc. found out about this it informed the Hoboken team that either Maria would have to go or the team would be out of the league. The National Office informed Hoboken that their charter, which had been approved by the United States Congress in 1964, stated that Little League was for boys only. The New Jersey team gave in to the National Office, so that not all the players would have to suffer the same fate as Maria Pepe. The National Organization for Women (NOW) stepped in to challenge Little League Baseball.

Little League Cases

On November 7, 1973, Hearing Officer Sylvia B. Pressler, ordered Little League Baseball, Inc. to admit girls ages eight to 12 for participation in its baseball programs in the state of New Jersey. Pressler stated,

> It is my understanding that Little League Baseball is a monumentally successful organization. . . As American as the hot dog and apple pie. There is no reason why that part of Americana should be withheld from little girls. The sooner little boys begin to realize that little girls are equal and that there will be many opportunities for a boy to be bested by a girl, the closer they will be to better mental health (NOW, 1974).

Dr. Creighton J. Hale, Executive Vice President of Little League and its Director of Research, a qualified physiologist, testified that in bone strength, muscle strength, and reaction time, girls were inferior to boys, thus increasing their risk of injury. The superior court, appellate division, held that,

> evidence permitted the finding that girls of the particular age class were not subject to materially greater hazard of injury while playing baseball than boys of the same age group, that a ball field at which tryouts are arranged, instruction given, practice held, and games played is a place of public accommodation, and that the organization was not within statutory exemption (NOW, 1974).

The Little League Baseball, Inc. defense also pointed out that in its Federal charter, the development of qualities of citizenship, sportsmanship, and manhood would be impaired if girls were allowed to play. The superior court found nothing of substance in the record to justify that the training of boys would suffer if girls were admitted. However, the decision on the appeals level was not unanimous. Judge J.A.D. Meanor, dissented, and in his dissent found nothing unreasonable about the position of Little League not wanting to teach young girls the skills of a sport that they would have no use for later in life. Judge Meanor felt that it would be reasonable to channel women into areas where they could maximize long term enjoyment (NOW, 1974). The only problem with Judge Meanor's rationale is that in 1972 Youth Sports, it was Little League Baseball or nothing for most American children. There were very limited alternatives for young girls in sport during the 1960s and early 1970s.

Almost one year later, a second case involving Little League Baseball, Inc., and its refusal to allow girls to participate went against the National Organization again. In the spring of 1974, ten year old Alison "Pookie" Fortin and her father went to Slater field in the City of Pawtucket, Rhode Island to sign up for the Darlington Little League. Alison met all of the eligibility requirements, except that she was a girl. After Allison was told that she could not play, she and her father brought suit. The lawsuit claimed that since the local little league played on public recreational facilities, that to deny their daughter the opportunity to use public-funded ball fields, would violate the equal protection clause of the Fourteenth Amendment. The United States District Court denied relief, but the plaintiffs appealed and the court of appeals reversed and remanded. The court of appeals held that:

> Little League organizations heavy and preferred dependency upon city baseball diamonds introduced significant state involvement in its activities sufficient to subject it to the equal protection clause; and that finding that injury would undoubtedly occur owing to the physical differences between boys and girls was unsupported and did not constitute a convincing factual rationale for the sex-based classification (*Fortin v. Darlington Little League*, 1975).

Little League Charter Amended

While the appeal was being argued, the United States House of Representatives amended the Federal Charter of Little League Baseball, Inc., to allow girls to participate on an equal basis with boys. Faced with twenty-two class action lawsuits filed across the country against Little League, the National Organization petitioned Congress to amend its Federal charter to include girls. One side note, during the trial phase of the case the president and coaches of Darlington Little League testified to a belief that girls would detract from the game; might cause boys to play less aggressively and more protectively; had a lower boiling point; would be more prone to injury, and if in need of first aid, would embarrass the male coaches; and would prefer to play with other girls. When Congress amended the Charter of Little League to allow girls to participate, the court of appeals asked

both sides if the question was now moot. However, the Darlington Little League Organization saw no reason to change the status quo and so the lawsuit continued, until March 31, 1975 when the decision went in favor of Allison Fortin (*Fortin v. Darlington Little League*, 1975).

These two landmark decisions went in favor of the rights of girls to play Little League baseball, but it did not put an end to the controversy or an end to the litigation. In *Magill v. Avonworth Baseball Conference*, ten year old Pamela Magill was not allowed to play baseball because of her gender. Magill's parents brought action against the non-profit corporation which operated the baseball conference, claiming that their daughter had been unconstitutionally discriminated against based on her sex. The District Court for Western Pennsylvania held that there was not state action and no unconstitutional discrimination and the United States Court of Appeals affirmed that decision. The Avonworth Baseball Conference was not affiliated with Little League Baseball, Inc., and when Little League changed to allow girls to participate, Avonworth did not. The trial court held that: "it is neither the intention of 1983 nor the purpose of the Fourteenth Amendment to circumscribe totally the individual liberties and freedoms of the private sector" (*Magill v. Avonworth Baseball Conference*, 1975). The league was a volunteer, private organization designed to furnish an athletic program for residents of a certain area and was not working on behalf of a municipal government. Since there was no state action, there was no violation of the Fourteenth Amendment and the defendant baseball league was within its rights to restrict play to one gender. The United States Court of Appeals affirmed that Pamela Magill had no constitutional right to play baseball in the Avonworth Baseball Conference.

National Organization Revokes Charter

In the case of *King v. Little League Baseball, Inc.* the girls lost again. Twelve-year-old Carolyn King of Upsilanti, Michigan wanted to play Little League baseball, but she was not allowed to because she was a girl. King's father brought action for injunctive relief under the Civil Rights Act to protect his daughters rights to the Fifth and Fourteenth Amendments. The local league voted to allow Carolyn to play but the National Organization revoked the charter of the League. By revoking the local Little League Charter, the National Organization meant that:

1. The local league's insurance would be canceled.
2. The local league's champion team could not play any other teams from chartered league.
3. The local league's all-stars could not play in the district tournament.
4. The local league's all-star team would not be eligible for the Little League World Series.
5. The local league's uniforms, equipment, bank account, etc., could be taken away.
6. The local league could not use Little League designation on its uniforms, stationary, fund drives, or other things (*King v. Little League Baseball*, 1974).

To put this in religious terms, the local little league would be excommunicated from the National Organization. District Judge Ralph M. Freeman dismissed the action, holding that there was not sufficient state involvement in the defendants "no girls" rule to bring it under color of state law. The district court ruled that it did not have jurisdiction over the subject matter of the case, and the court of appeals affirmed (*King v. Little League Baseball*, 1974).

The last baseball case to be reviewed is a 1983 decision, *McDonald v. New Palestine Youth Baseball League*. Kelly Joanna McDonald sought a preliminary injunction to be allowed to play boy's baseball instead of girl's softball. The basis for the lawsuit was that the New Palestine Youth Baseball League had violated McDonald's constitutional rights of association due to her gender. The district court held that there was no state action, or compelling state interest and that the girl would not succeed on the merits of her civil rights claims, and the court denied the preliminary injunction. The district court held that the league was not performing a government function, there was no state action involved, and the court held no jurisdiction over the parties or the subject matter of the case. In the final judgment, both sides had to pay their own attorney's fees and the cost of court was to be paid by the plaintiff (*McDonald v. New Palestine Youth Baseball League*, 1983).

Two landmark cases that said girls had to be allowed to play baseball with the boys, and three less famous cases stated it was up to the league to determine eligibility. The central theme in all the cases, is whether or not the baseball league's are performing a state action. I believe that these cases are a good representative of the history of gender equity in Youth Sport and show what the issues were and the bias in the late 1960s and early 1970s, about women in athletic competition. With the advent of Title IX, in non-contact sports, these cases have become a moot point of law. Girls today are being allowed to participate in most non-contact sports, and there is no gender equity issue like we had 20 years ago. With high school and colleges giving women opportunities for advanced athletic competition, local, city and community recreation departments and youth leagues are providing more and more opportunities to play. Where once we had a team for boys, now we have coed teams and single-sex teams allowing participants to make the decision on where to play. A coed team is better for females than no team, but two teams segregated by gender affords twice as many young people the chance to play. I believe that Title IX has created more opportunities on the youth level because women have more opportunities on the interscholastic and intercollegiate levels. Women today have their own teams, their own sports, like fast-pitch softball, field hockey, basketball, and soccer. If high school and college sports are not coed, why should they be coed on the youth level. Title IX is about opportunity, about equality, and today that means separate but equal sporting experiences. Women's sports today may be at the 1896 level of *Plessy v. Ferguson* that race was 100 years ago, and in the next century we may reach the point of *Brown v. Board of Education* of 1954 where separate will no longer be equal. At this point in time, especially in non-contact sports, separate and equal is good, because it gives twice the opportunities for young boys and girls.

Contact Sport Cases

There have been several Youth Sport cases in contact sports involving the issue of gender equity. In *Clinton v. Nagy*, a 12-year-old girl wanted to play recreational league football but was denied the opportunity because of her gender. The plaintiffs sought to use the Constitution, and the Fourteenth Amendment to gain the opportunity to play football. The court held that when a regulation or policy is based on a sex-based classification, the policy must undergo strict scrutiny under the equal protection clause of the Fourteenth Amendment. The court ruled that the policies, practices, and customs of the recreational league were in violation of the Constitution, and the case was decided in favor of the female (*Clinton v. Nagy*, 1974).

In the case of *Junior Football Association of Orange County, Texas v. Gaudet*, a trial court granted a temporary injunction to allow a girl to play football until she reached puberty. The decision was based on the Texas Constitution which provides: "Equality under the law shall not be denied or abridged because of sex, race, color, creed, or national origin." (*Junior v. Gaudet*, 1976) The Junior Football Association appealed the temporary injunction on the grounds that there was no state action sufficient to warrant the injunction. The temporary restraining order was reversed and dissolved, because the court of appeals did not find state action or private conduct closely interrelated in function with state action (*Junior v. Gaudet*, 1976). Another 12-year-old girl in the Chicago Park District wanted to play football in *Muscare v. O'Mallery*. Even though there was a touch football league for girls, the court held that touch football and tackle football were not the same game. Since there was no equivalent sporting experience for females, the league policy was a violation of the equal opportunity rights of the Fourteenth Amendment to the U.S. Constitution (*Muscare v. O'Malley*, 1977). Three football cases and two different rulings and the issue is whether or not the organization was a state actor. In *Clinton* and in *Muscare*, action was brought against two public recreation departments that sponsored football and the plaintiffs were successful The Texas case involved a private organization and the defendants won. These three cases seem to say that the Constitution protects people more against public agencies and organizations than it does against private organizations.

Soccer League Allows Females

One soccer case of note is *Simpson v. Boston Area Youth Soccer, Inc.* where a talented female wanted to play on the all-male soccer team. The Boston Area Youth Soccer, Inc. maintained a girls league and league officials felt that the plaintiff should play in that league. The plaintiff, however, contended that the girls league would give her inferior competition and was also not accessible. The case was settled out of court when the soccer league agreed to change its constitution to allow females to play on male teams and the mixed teams would still be entered into the boys league (Wong, 1994). This case does not establish any points of law, because it was

settled, but it does demonstrate that compromise and handling each situation on a case by case basis could help save legal expenses. The girl was an above average player, who was looking for a higher level of competition, to improve her skills, and to let her play on the boys team would probably not have opened up the flood gates of other females wanting to participate in the male league. Gender equity is about giving boys and girls the same opportunities to participate in a sporting experience. However, as boys and girls become older, success in sport becomes more about talent, because it is talent that allows people to be successful. If an athlete has talent, then that athlete should be allowed to maximize that talent against the best possible competition available.

Boxing Match Sanctioned

In 1982, in *Lafler v. Athletic Board of Control*, the Board of Control denied a female application to box in the flyweight division of the Golden Gloves Boxing Competition. The court cited Title IX regulations and the Amateur Sports Act as permitting the establishment of separate teams for males and females in contact sports (*Laffler v. Athletic Board of Control*, 1982). In October of 1996, Dallas Malloy became the first American female to put on gloves in a sanctioned amateur boxing match. It took a temporary injunction against USA Boxing to end the 106-year-old policy of men only in the ring. Malloy, 16, a light-weltweight, boxed Heather

Payner, a 21-year-old student, thanks in part to the American Civil Liberties Union that took up her case to box (Balzer, 1995).

In boxing, wrestling, football, and other contact sports, some females just want to try and see what they can do. Contact sports for safety reasons probably should stay segregated, but if a female wants to play, the best policy may be to let them try, instead of going to court and maybe still losing. Again we need to use common sense and a case by case approach. Take for instance 12-year-old Melissa Raglin of Boca Raton, Florida. Melissa had been a catcher for two and a half years on a coed baseball team when she was banned to the outfield for not wearing an athletic supporter and protective cup. "But she's not going to wear a boy's cup over a penis she doesn't have," according to Melissa's mother, Patricia Raglin (Pacenti, 1997). Even though Babe Ruth Officials stated that they were treating both sexes equally, a little common sense could have prevented this story from making the talk show headlines across the country. The sad part of the story was the damage done to the self esteem of some of the other players. One quote in the story was: "She doesn't want to play the outfield. That's where they put girls who can't play." I wonder how some of the girls and even some of the boys in the league who play the outfield felt after reading that quote. Again, common sense could have defused this situation before it ever got out of hand.

Reverse Gender Equity

The last case is a reverse gender equity case. In *White v. Corpus Christi Little Misses Kickball Association*, a ten-year-old boy wanted to play in the girls kickball league. The young boy was denied the opportunity to participate because of his gender, which he claimed was a violation of equal protection under the State and Federal constitutions. The district court ruled in favor of the Kickball Association and on appeal the claim was denied because of the failure to establish state action. Participation was denied the boy, by a private organization that was acting without any connection to the government (*White v. Corpus Christie*, 1975).

It appears from these different cases that public, tax supported city and county recreation departments are state actors, and therefore can not discriminate against boys and girls based on gender. However, a strictly private organization, even using public facilities, may limit membership and the opportunity to participate. A good parallel would be Virginia Military Institute, a state supported University in Virginia that has been forced to admit women. If a private college wished to remain single sex then that college would have the option, but a publicly funded college cannot discriminate based on gender.

Non-Discrimination Guidelines for Youth Sport

Parents want their children to have opportunities in sport, and they want those opportunities to be as equal as possible. Many mothers who were not allowed to play team sports when they were young, do not want their daughters missing out on the experience. Using Title IX as it applies to high schools and colleges as the model, it is possible to develop some non-discriminatory guidelines for Youth Sport such as:

1. First, public and private athletic associations should not discriminate based on gender. Athletic opportunity should be for everyone.
2. If there are separate teams based on gender, the teams should receive equal publicity about sign ups and registration.
3. All teams should have access to facilities and practice times. Maintenance and upkeep of facilities should be equal.
4. Uniforms and equipment should be of equal quality and cost.
5. Length of seasons, number of contests played, length of games, and policies about participation should be the same.
6. All-Star teams, travel teams, and post season competition should be available on an equal basis.
7. Awards, trophies, and certificates of participation should be comparable.
8. Administrators should place the same emphasis on recruiting coaches and officials for both teams.
9. Umpires and officials should be paid the same for the same type of work.
10. Cost for players to participate on teams or in leagues should be the same (Dougherty, 1994).

Separate teams as long as they are really equal is probably better and gives more children more opportunities. What we have to prevent is treating one gender like second class citizens, and Youth Sport is a good place to begin, to treat the genders equally. In 1973, Bill Gilbert and Nancy Williamson writing in *Sports Illustrated* gave several reasons why women should be able to participate in sport:

> Women who have had the regular experience of performing before others, of learning to win and to lose, of cooperating in team efforts, will be far less fearful of running for office, better able to take public positions on issues in the face of public opposition. By working toward some balance in the realm of physical activity we may indeed begin to achieve a more wholesome democratic balance in all phases of life (Appenzeller, 1975).

Sport and athletic competition is important, and as a society we need to encourage participation not practice elimination. Girls and women have made great progress since Title IX was passed in medicine, law, science, the military, and especially sport. Thanks to the Cindy Lowery's of another era, the possibilities for women in sport today are endless. Cindy Lowery James is currently a physical education teacher at Wingate Elementary School and in 1996–1997 was selected as her school's Teacher of the Year.

After the Facts

It is nothing new for a girl to play Little League Baseball. Girls have been playing baseball with boys for at least 20 years and several have proven themselves to be just as good at the game as their male counterparts.

Every now and then, a girl comes along and not only keeps up with the boys, but simply outplays them. Weddington Middle Schooler Cassie Palmer fits that example.

Palmer, a 12-year-old seventh grader, is quite comfortable in the male-dominated world of baseball. She's one of the top players in the Matthews Little League and proved it by throwing a one-hitter in a 2-0 win against a previously unbeaten, first-place team last week.

That win lowered Palmer's ERA to a scant 0.38 and gave her team a share of first place in its six-team division. Her team, Farm Bureau Insurance (FBI), is 7–1 in its division, 10–4 overall. Her pitching record is 4–1.

"We're the only team that beat them," Palmer said. "I was just having a good day pitching."

But there's more to Palmer than just throwing fastballs past her league's top hitters. She's hit four home runs—including a two-run blast in the first inning Saturday that was the difference in a 2–1 win—and sports a lofty .550 batting average.

Palmer, who stands taller than all of her teammates despite being one of seven 12-year-olds on the 13-and-under team, is not the only girl on her team. Christina Kemp plays first base.

But girls playing in Matthews Little League is not exactly a common occurrence. Palmer's coach, Steve Hands, who has coached in the league for 10 years, said he's only seen one other girl play baseball with the boys.

He said Palmer, who plays shortstop when she's not pitching, has played on a high level since she started on his team two years ago.

She batted .500 last year and will most likely be on the all-star team when this season ends.

"She's blended in with the team. They've accepted her," Hands said. "She's the team leader. They don't see her as a girl. They see her as an athlete."

Matthews Athletic Association also offers softball, but Palmer chose baseball. She's no stranger to softball, having played shortstop for the powerful Weddington Middle School softball team, which breezed through its season unbeaten against several Charlotte private schools.

She prefers baseball to softball because of the faster pitching. Hitting a fastball thrown overhand presents more of a challenge than a lot of the fast-pitch softball she's faced so far.

"(Baseball's) faster than softball," Cassie Palmer said. "Softball's just too slow. It's just not as fun playing with a big ball."

Palmer started playing baseball in the backyard with her father and her brother. She was 5-years-old at the time and surprised her father with how she could catch and throw.

"We'd throw the ball to her backhand and she could catch it," Tom Palmer recalled. "We knew there was something there."

That something eventually helped Palmer blossom into a solid three-sport athlete. Cassie said the boys accept her as a player and treat her with respect.

"I've played with most of them before," she said. "They accept me for who I am and not as a girl. They consider me part of the gang."

Palmer also plays the wing on an AAU basketball team, the Charlotte Fire, that plays in a tournament in Asheville next weekend. In July, her team travels to Orlando, Fla., for the national tournament.

She's the youngest player on the team.

"We're not going to be playing every day, so we're going to Disney World," Palmer said. "It should be fun."

Her father also proudly points out that Palmer carries a 94 average at Weddington Middle and even does a little babysitting.

"She even helps take care of her sister," her father Tom Palmer said. "She's like a second mom" (Behr, 1999).

References

Appenzeller, Herb. *Athletics and the Law*. The Michie Company, Charlottesville, Virginia, 1975.

Balzer, John. "Striking a Blow for Equality," *Los Angeles Times*, October 18, 1975.

Behr, Steve. "Palmer's Just Part of the Gang," *Monroe Enquirer Journal*, May 23, 1999.

Clinton v. Nagy, 411 F. Supp. 1396 (Ohio, 1974).

Coakley, Jay J. *Sport in Society*. Mosby Year Book, Inc., St. Louis, Missouri, 1994.

Dougherty, Neil J., David Auxter, Alan S. Goldberger, and Greg S. Heinzmann. *Sport, Physical Activity and the Law*. Human Kinetics, Champaign, Illinois, 1994.

Dworkin, Susan. "Fear Strikes Out," *MS*, vol. 2, p. 20, May 1974.

Fortin v. Darlington Little League, Inc., 514 F. 2d. 344 (Rhode Island, 1975).

Junior Football Association of Orange County Texas v. Gaudet, 546 S.W. 2d. 70 (Texas, 1976).

King v. Little League Baseball, Inc., 565 F. 2d. 264 (Michigan, 1974).

Lafler v. Athletic Board of Control, 536 F. Supp. 104 (Michigan, 1982).

Magill v. Avonworth Baseball Conference, 516 F. 2d. 1328 (Pennsylvania, 1975).

McDonald v. New Palestine Youth Baseball League, 561 F. Supp. 1167 (Indiana, 1983).

Muscare v. O'Malley, N.D. Illinois, 1977.

National Organization for Women v. Little League Baseball, Inc., 381 A. 2d. 33 (New Jersey, 1994).

Pacenti, John. "Girl 12, Refuses to Wear Boys Cup," *Charlotte Observer,* May 22, 1997.

Simpson v. Boston Area Youth Soccer, Inc., Superior Court, Massachusetts, 1983.

White v. Corpus Christie Little Misses Kickball Association, 526 S.W. 2d. 766 (Texas, 1975).

Wong, Glenn. *Essentials of Amateur Sports Law.* Second Edition. Praeger, Westport, Connecticut, 1994.

Wong, Glenn and Dan Covell. "The Rights Thing," *Athletic Business,* vol. 19, no. 4, April 1995.

Chapter 9

Persons with Disabilities

The only thing we have to fear is fear itself.
Franklin Roosevelt

Harold James: A Special Athlete

Growing up in Greensboro, North Carolina, I remember watching a football and track athlete at Guilford College named Harold James. I was in elementary school when Harold was at Guilford, and he was a very gifted athlete and had a remarkable career at the Quaker College. What made James special was that he had a shriveled up right leg, the result of polio as a child. Harold James set several school and conference records in track and became the starting quarterback in football, but he never thought of himself as handicapped. Just like Jim Abbot in baseball, and Kenny Walker in professional football, Harold James thought of himself as an athlete, a competitor. What I came to realize about Harold James, and what the world knows about Abbot and Walker is that they are more than athletes, they are winners, and we need winners in our society.

War-Caused Disabilities

Franklin D. Roosevelt is the only American in history to be elected President of the United States four times. Leader of our country through the Great Depression and World War II, Roosevelt was our first and so far only President to serve in the Oval Office confined to a wheelchair. Roosevelt was inflicted with polio at the age of 39 in 1921, and yet he overcame this crippling disease to lead the nation. Although Americans overwhelmingly accepted Franklin Roosevelt and elected him to the highest office, we have not been as eager to accept young athletes with disabilities into sport. Americans have traditionally looked for reasons to exclude

117

people with disabilities from competition, instead of looking for ways to include these young people in the sporting experience. There have been two major developments in this century that have begun to alter the approach to dealing with individuals with disabilities. First, we have had wars, Korea, Vietnam, Desert Storm, Kosovo and numerous other military actions that have taken healthy American men and women and returned them with disabilities. Soldiers, men and women, through no fault of their own, but who made the sacrifice to defend this country and they paid a price. Gradually over time we as a nation have come to the reality that wounded soldiers deserve more than our thanks, they deserve our help and assistance.

A Blind Golfer's Story

Charlie Boswell holds a record for a score of 81 for eighteen holes of golf in a national competition. His score may seem insignificant until you realize that his record came in a tournament sponsored by the United States Blind Golfers Association. Boswell has won twelve national titles in twenty years and scored a hole-in-one on a par three, 147 yard hole in Birmingham, Alabama.

While Charlie Boswell's story is unique, his accomplishments are typical for many individuals who continue to overcome adversity to bring attention to the potential in sports for people with handicapping conditions.

Charlie Boswell was an All America football player at the University of Alabama in the mid-1930s with a future in professional baseball. He commanded a tank battalion in North Africa during World War II and was blinded when his tank took a direct hit. At Valley Forge Rehabilitation Hospital in Pennsylvania, Boswell exhibited a belligerent and negative attitude, feeling sorry for himself with a "what's the use of living" philosophy. He refused to take part in the sports program at the hospital until a staff member told him that he was going to play golf the next day. Boswell who had never played a game of golf, replied, "What in the hell can a blind man do on a golf course?" The staff member told him, "Shut up, we're going."

Someone put a golf club in his hands the following day and guided him through some preliminary swings. Finally Boswell, after some practice swings on his own, hit his first tee shot ever. According to Boswell, "he hit the ball right between the screws and he could feel it going 250 yards right down the middle." Golf gave him a thrill he had never experienced and it became his rehabilitation and road back to an active life. He often questions what would have happened to him if he had missed his first swing (Appenzeller, 1983).

Second, and partly as a result of war, medical technology has improved so much, that people are able to live with and survive more severe dis-

abilities than ever before. The heroic struggle of Christopher Reeves, Superman, injured in a horseback riding accident, is an example of modern medical science and the will to survive. Injuries that in the past meant almost certain death, now mean life but with a disability. When a Christopher Reeves suffers a catastrophic injury, collectively we all realize that it could happen to us. Life can change very quickly.

Sports for Rehabilitation

In his 1952 State of the Union Address, President Dwight D. Eisenhower was the first Chief Executive to focus attention on a rehabilitation program for the disabled. Using sports as a way to rehabilitate injured soldiers began after World War II, and Eisenhower as a former military commander had an interest in the welfare of his former soldiers, when he spoke of the disabled. Over the last 45 years since that State of the Union Address, American have become more tolerant of persons with disabilities and more accepting of their desire to participate in sport. One of the reasons for widespread acceptance today has been Congressional legislation that has given rights and power to people with mental and physical disabilities. I believe that there have been five pieces of legislation that have had the greatest impact on turning the United States into a more inclusive society.

Legislation Passed for Persons with Disabilities

First in 1968, Congress passed Public Law 90-480, the Architectural Barriers Act, which began the policy of making public buildings accessible to everyone. Next came Public Law 93-112, the Rehabilitation Act of 1973 which was followed in 1975 by Public Law 94-142, the Education for All Handicapped Children Act. These three acts of Congress, changed forever the make up, enrollment and mission of public education in America. Not only were high schools affected, but when you talk about high schools, you are talking about interscholastic sport, a major component of the extracurricular experience. Public Law 93-112 and Public Law 94-142 introduced the concept of mainstreaming to America, and providing a free and quality education for every child, regardless of the disability. Another significant change over the last twenty years has been how we talk about people. We have gone from talking about handicapped children to children with a disability, or children with a disabling condition. We have gone from the mind set of children being handicapped, to one of children being exceptional or challenged but not handicapped. We handicap race horses, children have disabilities. Just the change in terminology speaks volumes about where we have come from and where we are going in this country.

The first three laws changed our facilities and education, the 1978 Amateur Sports Act changed the way we look at sport, particularly our Olympic movement. The Amateur Sports Act for the first time recognized athletes with disabilities as part of the Olympic movement. The eighth goal of the United States Olympic Committee states: " to encourage and provide assistance for athletic activities for women, individuals with disabilities and athletes of racial or ethnic minorities" (Dougherty, 1994).

Americans with Disabilities Act

In July of 1990, President George Bush signed the fifth major piece of legislation, the Americans with Disabilities Act (ADA) Public Law 101-336. Called the Civil Rights Act for people with disabilities, the ADA extended the rights of people with disabilities into the private sector and protected a wide range of individuals with disabling conditions. Some of the main provisions of the ADA in regard to sports and athletes are:

1. Prohibits discrimination in public accommodations.
2. Requires reasonable accommodations for the disability.
3. Requires that public accommodations that provide sport and physical activity make reasonable accommodations to include disabled citizens.
4. Requires integration to the maximum extent possible.
5. Requires adaptations to make programs accessible.
6. Sets standards for personnel who conduct programs in which the physical activity is not well defined.
7. Provides for monitoring by the Office of Civil Rights. (Dougherty, 1994).

ADA: Civil Rights Act for Disabled Persons

The ADA has been a very important piece of legislation for adults and children with disabling conditions. One of the far reaching segments of the law provides:

no individual shall be discriminated against on the basis of disability in the full and equal enjoyment of the goods, services, facilities, privileges, advantages, and accommodations of any place of public accommodation by any person who owns, leases, or operates a place of public accommodation (DePauw, 1995).

This section of the ADA covers where athletes practice, from school and university gymnasium, to local parks, stadiums and recreational facilities. The focus of the Americans with Disabilities Act is about more than just removing physical barriers, it means inclusion, making the effort to obtain universal participation. Individuals with substantial limitations of one or more life activities must be given access to YMCAs, YWCAs, Boys Clubs, and Little Leagues. The language of the ADA classifies individuals who have an impairment in walking, seeing, hearing, speaking, breathing, learning, or working as having a disability and as such are protected under the law. People with disabling conditions must be given the opportunity to participate in sport, unless their participation presents a direct threat to the health and safety of other participants. Sport is such an important part of society, that before an individual can be prohibited from participating, three criteria have to be met. To exclude someone based on the threat to health and safety factor, the threat must be real, it must be based on objective and unbiased information and all attempts must be made to reduce or eliminate the risk. The goal of the ADA is to include people in sport and recreation.

American Medical Association

In years past, it was the American Medical Association (AMA) that established standards and guidelines for the participation in contact and non-contact sports. The local family physician or team doctor using the AMA guidelines would make the call about who could play. Today programs and facilities have to be accessible to everyone and every effort must be made to include anybody that wants to participate. Now it is federal legislation and state and federal courts that are establishing the guidelines and making the decisions about who can try out and who can play. The Americans with Disabilities Act has done for children with disabilities what Title IX has done for women, and gender equity. Doors have been opened for more and more individuals. As we have learned with Title IX, there are still limitations on participation and there are still some who want to cling to the old way of doing things. Congress and the courts, it appears, prefer that parents and athletes be allowed to make the decision about whether to play or not instead of a coach, administrator, or doctor.

The Challenger Baseball Program

In the area of Youth Sport there are two main issues involving the right of children with handicapping conditions to participate. Do we have segregated programs for the disabled and non disabled or do we have one inclusive program for everybody. In 1987, Little League Baseball, Inc. threatened to lift the charter of the entire 32 team Brockton, Massachusetts Little League unless three teams of physically and mentally handicapped players were banned from competing. The National Organization of Little League stated that handicapped players were not covered by insurance and those players should be coached by professionals, and not volunteers. Little League Baseball, Inc. fought allowing girls to participate in the '70s, began in 1990 a challenger division for boys and girls with mental and physical disabilities

The Challenger Baseball program began with 300 children in five leagues, and within five years had grown to over 29,000 children participating in 820 leagues in the United States, Canada, and Puerto Rico. According to one parent whose son plays on a Challenger team, "These are just kids, they want to do kid things." However, for some, the Challenger Division is not enough, because others see discrimination and segregation in this type of league. Can we be separate and equal in sports? Valerie and Ronald Suhanasky of Milford, Connecticut do not want to see the Challenger program eliminated, but they are suing Little League Baseball, Inc. on behalf of their daughter Lauren. When Lauren's Challenger team wanted to play a regular team, they were told that the League Charter and insurance provisions would not allow it. The Suhanasky's want more opportunities for their daughter to play a comparable game (White, 1995). This issue is a difficult one to resolve, because some parents and athletes are happy with the Challenger Division as it is. Separate but equal is a common or case law issue, and I am not sure how it will be resolved.

Pony League Baseball

The case of *Shultz by and through Schultz v. Hemet Youth Pony League* is a typical case today. Geoffrey Shultz was born with spastic diplegia cerebral palsy, a condition which severely affects the muscles of his lower extremities causing them to spasm and contract. Geoffrey was able to walk, run, and play baseball with the assistance of crutches, and so in March of 1994 his father attempted to register his son to play baseball with Hemet Youth Pony League. Pony Baseball, Inc. Is a national non-profit corporation that serves as the administrative body for boys baseball and girls softball leagues. To be able to participate, a child has to be between 5 and 18 years of age, reside in the correct geographic boundaries, and pay the annual registration fee. At registration Geoffrey's father asked if his son would be allowed to play down in the nine to 10-year-old league, because the young Shultz had only played tee-ball. The local chapter inquired with the National Office and the National Office refused to let young Shultz play outside his legal age, because that would violate Pony Baseball rules. The basic issue in the lawsuit became:

> does a baseball program have to modify its traditional policies, rules and regulations to accommodate the needs of a child with a disability, in order to provide that child an opportunity to participate which is both appropriate for his needs as a person with a disability that substantially limits his mobility and equivalent to opportunities provided to his non-disabled peers (Schultz, 1996).

The answer in a word is, yes. The problem was that the defendants excluded the plaintiff without seeing him or knowing what he could or could not do. Geoffrey was excluded on the basis of assumed and unsubstanti-

ated concerns about possible risks of harm to the plaintiff, other players, and because of a lack of insurance coverage. By not attempting to determine the nature of Geoffrey's disability or the extent to which his disability could be accommodated, Pony Baseball, Inc. failed to fulfill its obligation under the Americans with Disabilities Act. Inclusion, not exclusion is the name of the new game, and every case, every situation must be examined individually, and decisions made based on the merits of the case. We should not predetermine what a child can or can not do.

Little League Baseball Challenges Coach in a Wheelchair

Larry Anderson, although confined to a wheelchair because of a spinal injury had been an on the field Little League Coach for three years. However, on July 24, 1991, President and Chief Executive Office, Dr. Creighton J. Hale of Little League Baseball, Inc. adopted a new policy on coaches:

(coach in a wheelchair) may coach from the dugout, but can not be in the coaches box. Little League must consider the safety of the youth playing the game, and they should not have the added concern of avoiding a collision with a wheelchair during their participation of the game (Anderson, 1992).

The local Little League refused to enforce the ban against Coach Anderson until the National Organization threatened revocation of charter and loss of tournament privileges. Anderson then filed a Civil Rights Action claiming that his exclusion from the field would violate the Americans with Disabilities Act. The Americans with Disabilities Act does not allow discrimination in areas of public accommodation and Little League Baseball, along with gymnasiums, health spas, bowling alleys, golf courses, and other places of exercise and recreation fall under the area of public accommodation. Even though discrimination is not allowed, there is nothing that requires a league or organization to let someone participate who is a direct threat to the health and safety of others. The court recognized that there is a need to balance the interest of people with disabilities against legitimate concerns for public safety, but that concern must be based on an individual assessment and not prejudice, stereotypes, and unfounded fear. The district court felt that Anderson's contribution of time, energy, enthusiasm, and personal example would be a benefit to the children, and that the plaintiffs work with young people teaches them the importance of focusing on the strengths of others and helping them rise to overcome personal challenges. The district court granted Larry Anderson the temporary restraining order so that he could continue to coach Little League Baseball.

When I was 11-years-old, the Guilford College Community of Greensboro, North Carolina started a local Little League Chapter. For two years, the best team in the league was the Yankees and they were coached by a man confined to a motorized cart. Charlie King, the coach, was born with a rare birth defect and his only means of locomotion was a three-wheeled cart that he drove all over the community. I had forgotten about Charlie King until I was writing this chapter and what I realized was that I did not even remember the name of my coach or any of the other coaches, but I remembered Mr. King. That was back in 1961 and 1962, back before the Civil Rights movement and Public Laws protecting the disabled. Nobody saw Charlie as a hero, or a pioneer, he was just a man who loved baseball and wanted to help some young boys more fortunate then him.

A Threat to the Game?

In Arizona, 14-year-old Nicholas Devlin was banned from the Elgin Eagles Soccer team by the Arizona Youth Soccer Association because he needed crutches to help him walk. Nicholas was born missing part of his lumbar spine and his disability requires him to use crutches to walk and run. When he plays soccer, Devlin can dribble the ball with his legs, but uses his crutches to pass the ball to other players. The Soccer League referee refused to allow Devlin to participate in a tournament in Tucson, and the League later barred Devlin from practicing or playing with his team. Attorney Steve Palevitz, with the Arizona Center for Disability Law, filed a lawsuit against the Soccer League alleging that the league had violated the ADA and the Arizona with Disabilities Act. The lawsuit demanded reinstatement and an unspecified amount of damages. The league referees said that using crutches would change the whole game of soccer, while Palevitz claimed that the crutches are the equivalent of legs, and that what Nicholas does is amazing (Corella, 1995). The question for the court will be whether or not Nicholas Devlin poses a threat to the health and safety of the other players. Let us admire the courage of a Nicholas Devlin, give encouragement, not seek to discourage and disqualify others like him from a big part of our culture, sport.

The Americans with Disabilities Act went into effect in 1993, and the other key legislation like Public Law 94-142 and Public Law 93-112 go back to the 1970s. With this legislative history, I do not anticipate a flood of lawsuits involving Youth Sport and children with disabilities. We have a few cases, but because of the legal mandates and programs like Special Olympics and Challenger Baseball, legal action may be held to a minimum. However, what does a Youth Sport coach, or administrator need to know in order to avoid violating the rights of disabled citizens. In the book, *Sport, Physical Activity and the Law*, the authors establish several management guidelines for intercollegiate and interscholastic sport and physical education. Using their guidelines plus legislative and case law we can modify the guidelines for Youth Sport.

General Guidelines for Youth Sport

1. Children and coaches with disabilities should be given the opportunity to participate in as many activities as possible.
2. A blanket policy that excludes groups or classes of people will not be acceptable. Decisions about participation must be made on an individual case by case basis.
3. Facilities and programs should be accessible to everyone and there should be an effort made to give participants an opportunity for success.
4. When necessary, accommodation should be made for the participant during try outs, practices and games. If special equipment is needed, it should be provided, as long as the activity is not altered or an unfair advantage is created.

5. All participants should have medical clearance from a doctor.
6. There should be a meeting of coaches, parents, officials, and the child to discuss all potential dangers and hazards to the child as well as to the teammates and opponents. If the individual with the disability creates a legitimate threat to the health and safety of others, then the individual can be refused the opportunity to participate.
7. Threat of injury to the individual with the disability is of concern, but is not a valid reason for exclusion. Inherent dangers of the sport should be explained to parent and child.
8. Alternative options such as Special Olympics, and Challenger Baseball should be discussed.
9. Discuss the situation with parents and children of the team. Keep people as informed as possible.
10. Remember that sport is about children and the children should be the first priority.
    These guidelines should make the sporting experience better for everybody.

HIV — AIDS Issues

There is one issue regarding the Americans with Disabilities Act and Youth Sport that has not been resolved . What happens when a child with the HIV infection wants to play a non-contact or a contact sport? What is the risk of exposure to the other players, coaches, officials, doctors, and trainers? Magic Johnson is the first big name superstar to participate knowingly while being infected with HIV, and even though he had a legal right to continue in the N.B.A. he chose to retire because of pressure form other players. Greg Louganus placed a doctor at risk when after suffering a bloody cut to the head, allowed the physician to treat him without adequate precautions or safety measures. Louganus knew he was HIV positive at the time but did not tell anyone. As the AIDS epidemic expands, Johnson and Louganus are but the tip of the iceberg, and this is a problem that coaches, administrators, doctors, and trainers are going to be faced with on every level. The American Academy of Pediatrics recommends the following policy regarding HIV and sports:

1. Athletes infected with HIV should be allowed to participate in all competitive sports.
2. A physician counseling a known HIV infected athlete in a sport involving blood exposure such as wrestling or football should inform him of the theoretical risk of contagion to others and strongly encourage the athlete to consider another sport.
3. The physician should respect the HIV infected athletes right to confidentiality. *This includes not disclosing patients infection status to the participants or staff of the sports program.* (Emphasis added.)
4. All athletes should be aware that the sports program is operating under recommendations 1 and 3.
5. Routine testing of athletes for HIV infection is not recommended (Risser, 1992).

HIV is a contagious, communicable disease with no known cure, and does pose a health threat to non-infected people. However, HIV infected individuals are listed under the Americans with Disabilities Act as a disabling condition and they are protected from discrimination. This is a difficult call, whether or not to let the child with AIDS compete in sports. For the parent who wants to see his/her HIV infected child enjoy as normal a life as possible, to the parent of the child that may be competing against the infected child in wrestling or football, the issue is not clear. What about the volunteer coach who may double as team trainer and has to administer first aid to a cut and bleeding player? Does that coach need to know if he has a player that is HIV positive? AIDS presents a dilemma in sports on the professional, college, high school, and youth level. How do you maintain confidentiality under law, and at the same time protect the health and safety of non-infected participants. The only incident of the AIDS virus being transmitted from one athlete to another during competition occurred several years ago in Italy during a soccer match when two players went to head a ball, and collided with each other and blood was exchanged. A rare chance, a freak accident, but an occurrence nevertheless.

In Virginia recently we had one of the first Youth Sport cases involving human immune deficiency virus (HIV) and a young infected athlete wanting to participate in a sport. Michael Montalvo was a 12-year-old boy that wanted to attend classes with his friends at a karate school in Colonial Heights, Virginia. The Southside Virginia Police Karate Association operated the U.S.A. Bushidokan karate school which taught combat-oriented martial arts. Michael enrolled in the school, but when it was discovered that he had aids, he was removed from the group activities. The young Montalvo was offered the opportunity to take private lessons but the family turned down that option and proceeded to bring legal action against the school. The plaintiffs charged that Michael was being discriminated against because of his disability and that he was protected under Title III of the Americans with Disabilities Act (ADA). The ADA allows people with disabilities access to public accommodations and the act states:

> no individual shall be discriminated against on the basis of disability in the full and equal enjoyment of the goods, services, facilities, privileges, advantages or accommodations of any place of public accommodation by any person, who owns, leases, or operates a place of public accommodation (*Montalvo v. Radcliffe*, 1999).

However, Congress did create a narrow exception to discrimination based on disability when it added that:

> a place of public accommodation is entitled to exclude a disabled individual from participating in its program where the individual poses a direct threat to the health and safety of others (*Montalvo v. Radcliffe*, 1999).

The Need to Protect the Public Health

The United States District Court for the Eastern District of Virginia and the United States Court of Appeals, Fourth Circuit, both ruled that the need to protect the public health outweighed the case of discrimination based on a disability. Because this style of martial arts involves body contact, sparring, and combat situations where injuries often occurs and blood flows freely, the court allowed Michael to be discriminated against. The ADA expects that there will always be a risk factor and that in normal situations every effort should be made to modify the activity, except where there is a significant risk to the health and safety of others. The court of appeals held that allowing a HIV student to participate in a combat style of karate would pose a significant threat to the health and safety of the other students. The severity of the risk was greater than normal, because aids is a fatal disease and there is no known cure.

A 12-year-old boy infected with the aids virus wants to learn karate with his friends. Michael Montalvo will not be the last young person who will want to play, although stricken with a deadly disease. The more lawsuits we have, the more court cases, the better guidelines we will have as far as who should and should not participate in youth sport with aids.

American Academy of Pediatrics Recommendations

1. Skin exposed to blood or other body fluids visibly contaminated with with blood should be cleaned as promptly as is practical, preferably with soap and warm water. Skin antiseptics (e.g., alcohol) or moist towelettes may be used if soap and water are not available.

2. Even though good hand-washing is an adequate precaution, water-impervious gloves (latex, vinyl, etc.) should be available for staff to use if desired, when handling blood or other body fluids visibly contaminated with blood. Gloves should be worn by individuals with nonintact skin. Hands should be washed after glove removal.

3. If blood or other body fluids visibly contaminated with blood are present on a surface, the object should be cleaned with fresh household bleach solution made for immediate use as follows: 1 part bleach in 100 parts of water or 1 tbsp bleach to 1 qt water, (hereafter called "fresh bleach solution"). For example, athletic equipment, (e.g., wrestling mats) visibly contaminated with blood should be wiped clean with fresh bleach solution and allowed to dry before reusing.

4. Emergency care should not be delayed because gloves or other protective equipment are not available.

5. If the care giver wishes to wear gloves and none are readily available, a bulky towel may be used to cover the wound until an off-the-field location is reached where gloves can be used during more definitive treatment.

6. Each coach and athletic trainer should receive training in first aid and emergency care and be provided with the necessary supplies to treat open wounds.

7. For those sports with direct body contact and other sports where bleeding may be expected to occur:
   A. If a skin lesion is observed, it should be immediately cleansed with a suitable antiseptic and securely covered.
   B. If a bleeding wound occurs, the individual's participation should be interrupted until the bleeding has been stopped and the wound is both cleansed with antiseptic and securely covered or occluded.

8. Saliva does not transmit HIV. However, because of potential fear on the part of those providing CPR, breathing (Ambu) bags and oral airways for use during cardiopulmonary resuscitation should be available in athletic settings for those who prefer not to give mouth-to-mount Resuscitation.

9. Coaches and athletic trainers should receive training in prevention of HIV transmission in the athletic setting; they should then help implement the recommendations suggested above (Risser, 1992).

These recommendations are a good guideline for all coaches and trainers who work directly with athletes. The risk of coaching someone that has grows every day as the aids epidemic expands.

The United States Congress has recognized that we have over 43 million Americans that are affected by some physical or mental disability. The time has come to open the doors of opportunity to the sporting experience to as many as possible and to find a new Franklin D. Roosevelt for the next generation.

After the Facts

There are kids who can't walk, ride a bike or even talk.

But at Misty Meadows Farm in Weddington, any kid can ride a horse.

Molly and Harry Swimmer, who own the farm, run a therapeutic riding program there for kids and adults with disabilities.

They call their equestrians Mitey Riders.

Horse-riding boosts their self-esteem and is good physical therapy for those with cerebral palsy, muscular dystrophy, spinal damage and other ailments that affect body movements.

As the horse walks, the rider feels the sensation in her own legs and hips. Riders strengthen their back muscles and improve balance by learning to sit tall on the horse.

On Saturday, about 90 riders put on an end-of-year show for their families. The program shuts down for three months in the summer.

Riders galloped around a dirt ring, stretched their arms in the air to demonstrate balance and guided their horses to walk over white poles lying on the ground.

Family members cheered from the sidelines, and after performing, each rider received a blue ribbon.

Jenna Clayton, 9, sat tall on a brown-and-white horse named Molly, which cantered around the ring as Jenna grinned widely.

Jenna was born with Down syndrome and only part of her esophagus. She's had 43 operations since birth.

"She got right on that horse and didn't turn back," said Jenna's mother, Mary. "It gives her something to look forward to each week."

Wesley Brower, 10, became a Mitey Rider three years ago. At the time, he couldn't stand up by himself and had to use a walker. He was quiet and withdrawn.

Now he walks around the grassy farm with a cane and can pull himself up to stand.

Wesley has taken drugs to strengthen his muscles, but grandfather Fred Brower attributes many of this grandson's improvements to riding.

The Swimmers started the Misty Meadows program after Harry put a family friend on a horse in 1994. Stacey Marx was 7 at the time, deaf and living with cerebral palsy.

Harry Swimmer, a former insurance executive, was drawn to the excitement he saw in the girl's face.

The Swimmers had bred and trained Saddlebred show horses on their farm for years. After seeing Stacey, they wanted to help more kids.

Harry studied therapeutic riding and started the program. Misty Meadows Mitey Riders, Inc. became an registered charitable organization in 1998.

The program runs nine months a year, three times a week. It's free to the children.

"The kids have done more for me than I could ever do for them," Harry Swimmer said.

"We see them improve. I don't know if it's from the riding or something else, but they have a smile on their face and that's all that counts" (Walker, 1999).

References

Anderson v. Little League Baseball, Inc., 794 F. Supp. 342 (Arizona, 1992).

Appenzeller, Herb. *The Right to Participate*. The Michie Company, Charlottesville, Virginia, 1983.

"Big League Dispute," *USA Today*, November 18, 1987.

Corella, Hipoliot R. "Soccer League is Sued to Let Cripple Boy Play," *Arizona Daily Star*, October 23, 1995.

DePauw, Karen P. and Susan Gavron. *Disability and Sport*. Human Kinetics, Champaign, Illinois, 1995.

Dougherty, Neil. *Sport, Physical Education and the Law*. Human Kinetics, Champaign, Illinois, 1994.

Krentz, Jeri F. "All Hits, No Errors in Kids Program," *The Charlotte Observer*, 1997.

Montalvo v. Radcliffe, 167 F. 3d 873 (4th Cir. 1999)

Risser, William L. "HIV and Sports," *The Physician and Sport Medicine*, vol. 20, no. 5, May 1992.

Schultz By and Through Schultz v. Hemet Youth Pony League, 943 F. Supp. 1222 (California, 1996).

Walker, Andrea K. "Mitey Riders Build Strength, Relish New Found Confidence," *The Charlotte Observer*, May 23, 1999.

White, Carolyn, "Small Players, Big Trouble," *USA Today*, August 17, 1995.

Chapter 10

Organizations and Administration

The transmission of morals is no longer safe in the family be-cause the activities out of which morals arise have been taken away.
Luther Gulick

Luther Gulick: A Social Pioneer

Luther Gulick, in the above quote, was talking about the lack of family values in America at the turn of the century. Gulick and many of the social pioneers of his day, saw non-profit organizations created to govern children and young adults as the solution to the problem of urbanization in the United States. The adult-directed youth sport movement reflected the concerns of citizens about the effects of economic and social change on the traditional child-rearing practices (Rader, 1996).

Youth Groups and Programs

The Young Men's Christian Association (YMCA) was founded in 1851 in England to offer advice and assistance to thousands of young men flocking to the newly industrialized cities of Great Britain. The YMCA was followed by the Boys' Club of America (1906), The Playground Association of America (1906), Boy Scouts (1910), Camp Fire Girls (1910), and Girl Scouts (1912) (Swanson, 1995), all organizations run and directed by adults but conducted for the purpose and benefit of children and young adults. These organizations incorporated recreational and sports activities into their curriculum in order to attract young men and women. Adult-directed youth sport type activities were a major component of the Social Reform movement that swept this country one hundred years ago. There was a belief that children needed something to take the place of growing up on the farm, where hard work and manual labor were part of life. Many leaders felt that sports could serve as a replacement for the rural environment, fill the void left by the disappearance of the household economy, the absence of the early work experience, the weakened authority of religion and the break down of small town life. These non-profit organizations helped train volunteers, provided newsletters, and established guidelines so that adults could provide positive educational experiences.

> Team sport offered an unparalleled opportunity for adults to encourage in boys the healthy growth of moral and religious reflexes. Stemming from the instinct for cooperation, team sports required the highest moral principles—teamwork—self-sacrifice, obedience, self-control, and loyalty (Rader, 1996).

Public School Athletic League

In 1903, Luther Gulick established the Public School Athletic League in New York City and in 1905 at the urging of President Theodore Roosevelt, the National Collegiate Athletic Association (NCAA) was founded to help govern college athletics. These two organizations were the first to attempt to regulate and govern athletic competition on the amateur level. The Public School Athletic League represented interscholastic competition, while the NCAA regulated intercollegiate competition. The 1920s, considered by historians to be the first Golden Age of Sports in America, saw an increase in the sporting culture and the development of several youth sport organizations. Where the YMCA, Boys Club, and Girl Scouts were seen as educational and social in context with sport as a secondary component, the new organizations had a primarily sport function. In 1924, the Cincinnati Community Service started a city baseball tournament for boys under the age of 13. The *Los Angeles Times* conducted a junior pentathlon in 1928, and the Southern California Tennis Association began in 1930. Also in 1930 the Catholic Youth Organization was founded and began basketball and boxing tournaments (Swanson, 1995). Milwaukee organized its kids baseball in 1936 and in 1939 *Life* magazine published a feature article on a boys football game in Denver. It was also in 1939 that the most famous national organization for youth sport was founded in Williamsport, Pennsylvania, Little League Baseball. With its mission to provide young boys, a major league type baseball experience, Little League became the model for all future national sports organizations. Little League Baseball, Inc. today has over 7,000 leagues worldwide, with 190,000 teams and over 2.9 million children participating annually (*Little League Baseball*, 1995). There are numerous national organizations today that govern and control youth sport participation from basketball to wrestling and every sport in between. Consider the following statistics as reported in 1997:

Over 500,000 boys and girls ages seven through 18 participated on 42,563 teams run by the American Youth Soccer Organization.

Two hundred fifty thousand boys and girls ages five to 16 participated on 4,500 tackle, 500 flag, and 3,900 cheer squads overseen by Pop Warner Little Scholars, Inc.

Nearly 200,000 boys and girls ages seven to 18 competed on basketball teams, and over 60,000 competed on swimming, wrestling, gymnastics, and track teams administered by the Amateur Athletic Union (AAU).

Membership in USA Hockey, includes approximately 294,000 boys and girls 17 years old and younger who participate on 21,000 teams.

Somewhere between 20 and 35 million youth participate annually in non-school sponsored sports.

1964 and 1974 Acts of Congress

These organizations function as private governing bodies outside of many government and constitutional restrictions. However, just like the NCAA, another private organization, many youth organizations have found themselves in costly litigation. Not all problems are solved in the neighborhood, but many of the disputes go from the local, to the regional, to the national level. In the case of *Little League Baseball v. Welsh Publishing Group*, the national scope of Little League was established. Little League Baseball was incorporated by an Act of Congress in 1964 and in 1974 the Act to incorporate was amended to include girls. The Act declares that the purpose of the Little League Corporation are:

1. To promote, develop, supervise, and voluntarily assist in all lawful ways the interest of young people who will participate in Little League Baseball.
2. To help and voluntarily assist young people in developing qualities of citizenship and sportsmanship.
3. Using the discipline of the native American game of baseball to teach spirit and competitive will to win, physical fitness through individual sacrifice, the values of team play, and wholesome well-being through healthful and social association with the youngsters under proper leadership (Masteralexis, 1998).

The powers of the corporation include suing and being sued in any court of competent jurisdiction in the United States. The Court in *Welsh* held that Little League Baseball, Incorporated, is a national citizen for the purpose of litigation. The *Welsh* case confirms that National Youth Sport organizations, like Little League Baseball, Inc. are national organizations and may operate throughout the United States, Puerto Rico and the other possessions of the United States. Being national in scope opens Youth Sport Organizations up to potential litigation on both federal and state levels.

Tarkanian v. NCAA

It is not uncommon for state and national sports organizations to become involved in personnel decisions and subsequent litigation. The NCAA several years ago established a precedent in the Jerry Tarkanian case. Jerry Tarkanian was the Men's Basketball Coach at the University of Nevada, Las Vegas (UNLV) who was suspended by the university for NCAA violations. Tarkanian sued the university and the NCAA claiming that he had been denied his rights to due process, as a state employee and a tenured professor. The Supreme Court of Nevada agreed that the NCAA even though a private organization was functioning as a state actor and thus was required to give Tarkanian due process. However, in December of 1988, the United States Supreme Court in *NCAA v. Tarkanian* reversed the judgment of the Nevada Supreme Court and ruled that the NCAA was not acting under color of Nevada law. The United States Supreme Court for the first time in history was asked to decide the fate of a college basketball coach. The Supreme Court came down on the side of the National Private Athletic Organization, and three cases, *Butler v. USA Volleyball, Cantrell v. U.S. Soccer Federation* (USSF) and *Christensen v. State Youth Soccer Association* demonstrate what organizations have to do to terminate a coach.

Volleyball Coach Sued

Rick Butler was a very successful junior volleyball coach, having coached almost 30 national championship junior girls teams, created the Great Lakes Center in West Chicago, a premier volleyball facility, operated the Sports Performance Volleyball Club, ran the largest national volleyball camp, and was the most published video author in volleyball (*Butler*, 1996). USA Volleyball however, received complaints from several former players alleging that Butler had sexual relationships with them when they were under 18 years of age and playing on his volleyball club. Butler was given two separate hearings, received notice of the specific charges of sexual misconduct and had copies of all the documents the Ethics Committee possessed. At the hearing, Butler had the assistance of legal counsel, was allowed limited cross examination of the complaints and was allowed to present witnesses who could testify as to the events in question. The

Ethics Committee expelled Rick Butler from USA Volleyball membership for life, with the option of applying for conditional membership in five years. Butler then brought legal action against USA Volleyball and the trial court granted his motion and permanently enjoined USA Volleyball from enforcing his expulsion. The trial court found that Butler had met all four prongs necessary to obtain injunctive relief:

1. a clear and ascertainable right in need of protecting;
2. irreparable harm without injunctive relief;
3. no adequate remedy at law;
4. success on the merits (*Butler*, 1996).

USA Volleyball appealed the trial court decision and the Appellate Court of Illinois reversed the trial court decision. The appellate court held that:

> Disciplinary proceedings conducted by voluntary associations do not require strict compliance with judicial standards of due process but rather accused member is entitled to hearing before fair and impartial tribunal; fair hearing assumes that accused member is given adequate notice of charges, has the opportunity to defend and same evidence must be presented at hearing to support alleged charges (*Butler*, 1996).

The appellate court added that courts are reluctant to interfere with the disciplinary actions of voluntary associations. Historically volunteer associ-

ations have been overruled in courts of law when: "association action violated the Constitution or bylaws of the association, when the association rules and proceedings violated concepts of fundamental fairness or when the association's action was motivated by prejudice, bias or bad faith." Disciplinary proceedings conducted by voluntary associations do not require strict compliance with judicial standards of due process. The appellate court ruled that an accused member is entitled to: a fair and impartial tribunal, notice of charges, and evidence of the charges. USA Volleyball gave Rick Butler a full and fair procedure and followed the Association's bylaws and operating code, and therefore was justified in expelling the coach from membership (*Butler*, 1996).

Soccer Coach Put on Probation

Don Cantrell was a youth soccer coach who was placed on probation and brought a lawsuit against the local, state, and national soccer association. Cantrell was the Coach of the Ione Soccer Club of the Frontier County Soccer Association which was a member of the Oklahoma Soccer Association (OSA) which was a member of the United States Youth Soccer Association (USYSA) and USYSA is a member of the United States Soccer Federation (USSF), the national governing body of the sport under the Amateur Sports Act of 1978 (*Cantrell*, 1996). The Oklahoma Soccer

Association received a complaint that Cantrell assaulted an official and he was placed on probation for two years, but allowed to continue to coach. Cantrell claimed that a hearing was conducted in violation of the Amateur Sports Act of 1978 and that the State Association violated its own rules and regulations. The Amateur Sports Act of 1978 authorized the United States Olympic Committee to recognize one national governing body for each Olympic or Pan American Sport. Each national governing body is then granted exclusive right to conduct amateur competition, establish procedures for eligibility, and provide procedures to handle disputes and grievances of the members.

National Governing Bodies

The Amateur Sports Act of 1978 gave legal recognition to the concept of international amateur athletic competition, and also recognized the National Governing Bodies (NGB) of the various sports as designated by the United States Olympic Committee (USOC) (Dougherty, 1994). Each National Governing Body is charged with nine specific duties:

1. to develop interest and participation throughout the United States and be responsible to the persons and amateur sports organizations it represents;
2. to coordinate with other organizations to minimize scheduling conflicts;
3. to take into account the opinions of amateur athletes in rendering policy decisions and keep the athletes informed of those policy decisions;
4. to promptly review requests of amateur sports organizations or other persons for sanctions to hold or sponsor competitions, within or outside the U.S.;
5. to allow athletes to compete in international amateur athletic competition conducted by the NGB;
6. to provide equitable support and encouragement for participation by women where separate programs for male and female athletes are conducted on a national basis;
7. to encourage and support amateur sports for individuals with disabilities and to expand opportunities for those individuals to participate in all athletic competition;
8. to render technical information on physical training, equipment design, coaching, and performance analysis; and
9. to encourage and support research, development, and dissemination of information in the areas of sports medicine and sports safety (The Amateur Sports Act of 1978).

The National Governing Bodies are specifically required by law to:

1. have as its purpose the advancement of amateur athletic competition and, to that end, be incorporated as a nonprofit corporation and maintain the wherewithal to fulfill its purpose;
2. submit a copy of its corporate charter and by-laws and such additional information as the USOC may require;
3. submit to arbitration any disputes as to eligibility of any athlete, coach, trainer, manager, administrator, or official or any disputes regarding its recognition as a governing body;
4. be a member of not more than one international sports federation that governs a sport played in the Olympic or Pan American Games and that exercises independent control over its sport;
5. demonstrate that membership is open to any individual or amateur sports organization in the sport governed;
6. refrain from discrimination on the basis of race, color, religion, age, sex, or national origin to provide equal opportunity to participate;
7. provide fair notice and opportunity for a hearing to any party before declaring him or her ineligible to participate;
8. be governed by persons who are selected to govern without regard to race, color, religion, national origin, or sex;
9. demonstrate that no less than 20% of the voting members of its governing board of directors are either actively engaged in amateur competition in the particular sport or have represented the U.S. in international athletic competition in the sport within the preceding 10 years;
10. provide for reasonable direct representation on its board that reflects "the nature, scope, quality, and strength of the programs and competitions of such amateur sports organizations in relation to all other programs and competitions in such sport in the United States" (36 U.S.C. 391);
11. demonstrate that none of its officers are also officers of any other NGB;
12 provide procedures for prompt and equitable dispute resolution;
13. have eligibility criteria relating to amateur status that are no more restrictive than criteria utilized by the corresponding international sports federation; and
14. demonstrate that it can meet all responsibilities imposed on NGB's by the law (Dougherty, 1994).

Cantrell claimed that he suffered pain, emotional distress, and humiliation as the result of the action of the Association, but the District Court of Oklahoma County ruled that the coach could prove no set of facts that would entitle him to relief. The court of appeals upheld the ruling of the trial court. In this situation a coach is placed on probation for assaulting an official and the coach believed that he has not been treated fairly. However, in court the coach was not able to prove that he was treated unfairly and thus lost the case. Courts traditionally do not like to become involved in the internal decision of private organizations. Where membership is voluntary, private organizations can establish and enforce their own rules and policies unless those rules or policies infringe on protected constitutional rights.

Coach Challenges Youth Sport Organization

Another example of a coach bringing a lawsuit against a youth sport association is *Christensen v. Michigan State Youth Soccer Association, Inc.* Mark Christensen brought suit seeking damages for breach of contract, tortuous interference with contractual relationship, fraud, and violations of constitutional due process. As the result of complaints regarding the plaintiff's behavior at several youth soccer league functions and following notice and a hearing, the coach was found to have violated the rules and regulations of the MSYSA, and he was suspended for a six-month period. Because of the suspension, Christensen was discharged from employment as Head Coach and Director of Player Personnel by the Detroit Wheels, a professional soccer club and in addition, an offer of employment with the Detroit Neon professional soccer team was withdrawn (*Christensen*, 1996). The circuit court denied Christensen's motion for declaratory judgment and granted summary judgment for the Association. The court of appeals held that:

> where a private association has provided a reasonably effective means of resolving controversies before it, and where there is no evidence of fraud by association in its treatment of the complaining members courts should not interfere with orderly governing of the association.

The court added:

> courts have no business regulating the procedures of private associations absent a compelling showing that substantial rights of a member are implicated and that there is no reasonable opportunity for the member to effectively assert those rights within the confines of the group.

Christensen also claimed that he was not afforded due process by the MSYSA when it imposed a six-month suspension followed by a six-month probationary period.

Private Associations and Due Process

The court again held that there is no provision of law that imposes the same procedural rules of due process upon private associations as on public entities. The court of appeals held that:

1. internal appellate procedure adopted by association was sufficient,
2. member was not excused from compliance with appellate procedures of association on ground that compliance would have been futile.
3. federal and state constitutional due process provisions were inapplicable to action of association.
4. even if they were applicable, they called only for notice and opportunity to be heard which had been provided.
5. failure to show injury from alleged misrepresentation made to member by association representative that suspension would not affect his soccer career precluded fraud claim (*Christensen*, 1996).

Youth Sport Organizations Sued for Participant Injuries

The previous cases represent Youth Sport Organizations and litigation involving personnel decisions. Youth Sport Organizations have also been named in lawsuits when injuries have occurred to participants and adult leaders. When baseball catcher William Rich was injured in a collision with an opposing player at home plate, his parents sued the Little League Corporation to recover damages (*Rich*, 1994). William's parents claimed that by assigning their son to the position of catcher, Little League unreasonably increased his risks of being injured. The West Shore Little League, Inc. established its defense based on the assumption of risk doctrine. The Supreme Court, Richmond County denied the corporations request for summary judgment, but on appeal, the Supreme Court Appellate Division reversed the lower court ruling and dismissed the complaint (*Rich*, 1994).

Volunteer's Death

Frances B. Holland brought suit against the North DeKalb Little League, Inc. for the death of her husband (*North DeKalb*, 1969). Mr. Holland was a member of the North DeKalb Boy's Club Athletic Association and was supervising and participating in the erection of a flag pole at the ball field. Holland was electrocuted when the flag pole touched a high voltage line. The Superior Court, DeKalb County, denied the Little League's motion for summary judgment and defendant appealed. The court of appeals held that the decedent had ignored several warnings that the wires were too close, shrugged off the warnings, and proceeded anyway. The court held: "It is apparent from the facts that the cause of death of the deceased was his lack of ordinary care for his own safety" (*North DeKalb*, 1969). The court of appeals added: "one who recklessly tests an observed and clearly obvious peril is guilty of a lack of ordinary care and his own negligence." The Court of Appeals granted North DeKalb Little League Inc. Motion for summary judgement, reversing the trial court decision (*North DeKalb*, 1969).

In *North Dekalb*, the volunteer was more liable or more negligent than the Little League Corporation. Even though Little League was not held negligent in this tragedy, the volunteer or next of kin still had the right to bring a lawsuit and seek damages.

Volunteer vs. Gratuitous Employee

The issue in *Bond v. Cartwright Little League Inc.* was whether the plaintiff was a volunteer or a gratuitous employee (*Bond*, 1995). James Bond was injured climbing a metal pole to remove stadium floodlights, purchased by Cartwright Little League, Inc. Cartwright Little League, Inc., an Arizona non profit corporation, purchased the stadium floodlights at auction from the Phoenix municipal stadium. The officers of the Little League decided to remove the lights with the help of volunteers, and James Bond was asked to volunteer at a general meeting of parents. Bond attempted to climb one of the metal poles, but approximately three quarters of the way up, he began to experience muscle spasms and decided to come down. Halfway down, Bond lost his grip, fell over 40 feet and was injured. The jury returned a verdict for the plaintiff in the amount of $100,000 and judgment was entered therein. The superior court granted defendant's motion for judgment notwithstanding verdict or the alternative motion for a new trial and the plaintiff appealed. Cartwright Little League contended that Bond was a mere volunteer to whom a very slight duty of care was owed, while Bond argued that he was a gratuitous employee, and a master-servant relationship existed, and therefore was owed a higher standard of care. The superior court held that "plaintiff was a gratuitous employee of corporation rather than a mere volunteer" (*Bond*, 1975). Cartwright Little League set the time and place as well as the manner in which lights were to be removed and had control over Bond's actions while he was working. What is a reasonably safe place to work, not only depends on the condition of the premises but also on the ability of the worker. The supreme court held that Cartwright Little League violated standards of reasonable care by:

1. failure to warn Bond of the danger in order that he could decline to work on the pole.
2. not determining that Bond was capable of climbing the pole (*Bond*, 1975).

A Question for the Jury

The supreme court ruled that whether corporation violated standards of reasonable care in failing to warn was a jury question and the trial court should not have granted motion for a new trial. The judgment notwithstanding was set aside, the order granting the motion for a new trial was set aside and the matter remanded to the trial court for entry of judgment on the verdict. Asking someone to volunteer or asking someone to do something specific creates a relationship between the two parties. Today when people volunteer, there is an expectation that the facilities will be safe and that people will be warned about dangerous or hazardous conditions. Failure to have safe facilities or failure to warn, then becomes issues for juries to determine, if and when litigation arises. Youth Sport Organizations that rely on volunteers to conduct activities have to make every effort to protect and ensure the safety of the volunteers. Not paying someone does not lessen the organization's responsibility to protect that person from unnecessary injury or harm.

In *Bowser v. Hershey Baseball Association*, a member of the baseball association brought personal injury action against the association (*Bowser*, 1986). John Bowser was a former baseball player and coach who, as commissioner of the "Teener" league, helped conduct tryouts. While standing in the area near the players bench, he was struck in the eye by a batted ball. Bowser argued that the Association had the task of running the tryouts and that he was a client or customer and therefore a business invitee and that the Association had a duty to protect him from foreseeable harm. The trial court held that there could be no recovery and entered a compulsory non-suit and the plaintiff appealed. The superior court held that:

1. member actively engaged in organizing and conducting try outs for associations baseball program could not recover damages for personal injuries suffered when struck by batted ball during try outs.
2. member voluntarily exposed himself to risk of being hit by batted ball.

3. association was not required to give warnings or take special precautions to protect members from batted ball (*Bowser*, 1986).

Bowser agreed to participate on the field and as a former player and coach knew the inherent risks of baseball. One of the risks of baseball is being hit by a batted ball, while falling down a light pole is not a normal risk and creates a different duty of care. The superior court added, the rule is that: "persons conducting the activity have no duty to warn or protect participants against risks which are common, frequent, expected, and inherent in the activity itself" (*Bowser*, 1986). The superior court affirmed the decision of the trial court in favor of the Hershey baseball Association.

In West Hartford, Connecticut the Youth Baseball League was sued by a father whose son was cut from the team and sent to the town's equivalent of the minors (*Boston Globe,* 1997). Peter Kelley, an attorney and former coach in the West Hartford Youth League, filed the lawsuit in May, after his 10-year-old son, Ryan was cut from the Exchange team. The 10-year-old was cut after two practices, causing him emotional distress and severe shock to his nervous system according to his father. This case has yet to reach the courts, but is another example of the type of lawsuit that a Youth Sport Organization may have to deal with.

Volunteer or non-profit, Youth Sports Organizations, whether on the local, state, or national level are not immune from litigation. When private organizations have established sound and fair guidelines, and have followed their own guidelines, courts have been reluctant to intervene. However, it is important that organizations have written rules and policies, and those policies are clearly enforced. All rules and policies should place the health and safety of the juvenile participant as the first priority.

One area where the courts have not been as reluctant to get involved has been issues involving the Americans with Disabilities Act, discussed in an earlier chapter. When organizations, public or private have been accused of discriminating against citizens protected by the ADA, the courts have been supportive of the individual over the organization. Youth sport organizations need to be aware of the children who are classified under the Americans with Disabilities Act, and every effort should be made at inclusion.

In the United States we have a heritage and rich tradition of private clubs and organizations, "member only" and that tradition will probably continue into the next century. However, private does not mean unconstitutional, and as long as private organizations seek to protect the rights of individual members, those organizations will be allowed self-government.

After the Facts

Twelve-year-old Melissa Raglin can't play catcher on her coed baseball team anymore. She doesn't wear the right equipment.

Melissa is refusing to obey a Babe Ruth League rule that she wear a jock strap and protective cup, because, well, she doesn't see the need.

"When the ump asked me if I was wearing a cup at the beginning of the second inning, I took my helmet off and said, 'I'm a girl,'" said Melissa, who sat behind home plate for two-and-a-half years—without a cup—until last Thursday.

Apparently Melissa, her coach and most of the umpires hadn't even realized that the rule that catchers must wear cups applied to girls, too. She has been banished to the outfield until she complies.

The dispute has become a hot topic in the community and on talk radio, drawing in the league's national officers and the National Organization for Women.

"It's almost some kind of harassment," said Linda Bliden, president of NOW's South Palm Beach County chapter. "The cup has nothing to do with a female anatomy. Why are they forcing girls to wear it?"

She wondered if boys would object if made to wear bras.

The Babe Ruth League said it is treating both sexes equally in requiring all catchers to wear a cup, a triangular concave piece of hard plastic that slips into a jock strap and is designed to protect male testicles from a foul ball or wild pitch.

Girls have been playing in the league—with 1 million participants nationwide—since the 1950s.

"It's for her protection," James Stewart, Babe Ruth's commissioner for the Southeast Region, said from Trenton, NJ. "A blow there to a young girl could have devastating long-term effects. It's no different than her mask."

But doctors said that girls do not need as much groin protection as boys do and that, in any case, girls should not wear gear designed for boys.

"I would not apply a boy's device to a girl—they're made for boys," said Dr. Francisco Medina, medical director of children's emergency at Baptist Children's Hospital in Miami. "Any extra protection would be good, yet it's probably not as important as in boys."

Stewart said she could play if she wears female protective gear—briefs with a padded crotch that can be ordered at sporting goods stores. But Melissa's mother, Patricia Raglin, said store clerks laughed at her when she inquired about such a product.

"If something was made for a girl, we'd have gotten it and she'd be wearing it," Raglin told the *Sun-Sentinel* of Fort Lauderdale. "But she's not going to wear a boy's cup over a penis she doesn't have."

Melissa, the starting catcher for the Boca Raton Youth League Dodgers, played outfield for two playoff games rather than wear a cup. Then, eager to catch in a playoff game Sunday, she showed up wearing her cup — on her ankle. League officials said she was mocking the rules and again exiled her to the outfield.

"She doesn't want to play the outfield. That's where they put girls who can't play," Raglin said. "The boys like her as catcher. They want her there."

By Wednesday, Melissa sounded as if she were ready to compromise. She has put in a rush order for female protective gear from Bike Athletic Co. of Knoxville, Tenn.

"If they'd let me catch, I'd probably put it on," Melissa said. "I just want the rule changed...I'm just trying to change this rule for everybody" (Pacenti, 1997).

References

American Sports Act of 1978.

Associated Press. "Father Sues After Son Cut From Team," *The Boston Globe,* June 4, 1997.

Bond v. Cartwright Little League, Inc., 536 P 2nd 697 (Arizona, 1975).

Bowser v. Hershey Baseball Association, 516 A 2nd 61 (Pennsylvania, 1986).

Butler v. USA Volleyball, 673 Northeastern 2nd 1063 (Illinois, 1996).

Cantrell v. U.S. Soccer Federation (USSF), 924 Pacific 2nd 789 (Oklahoma, 1996).

Christensen v. Michigan State Youth Soccer Association Inc., 553 N.W. 2d 634 (Michigan, 1996).

Dougherty, Neil J. *Sport, Physical Activity and the Law.* Human Kinetics, Champaign, Illinois, 1994.

Little League Baseball, Incorporated v. Welsh Publishing Group, 874 F. Supp. 634 (Pennsylvania, 1995).

Masteralexis, Lisa Pike. *Principles and Practice of Sport Management.* Aspen Publishers, Gaithersburg, Maryland, 1998.

North Dekalb Little League, Inc. v. Holland, 168 S.E. 2d. 169 (Georgia, 1969).

Pacenti, John. "Girl, 12, Refuses to Wear Boys Cup," *The Charlotte Observer*, May 22, 1997.

Rader, Benjamin. *American Sports*. Third Edition. Prentice-Hall, Englewood Cliffs, New Jersey, 1996.

Rich v. West Shore Little League Baseball, Inc., 618 N.Y. Suppl. 2nd 106 (New York, 1994).

Swanson, Richard and Betty Spears. *History of Sport and Physical Education in the United States*. Fourth Edition. Brown and Benchmark, Madison, Wisconsin, 1995.

Tarkanian v. NCAA, 109 S.Ct. 454 (1988).

Chapter 11

Sexual Abuse in Youth Sports

The average "preferential" molester, the kind most common in Youth Sports, victimizes about 120 children before he is caught.
(Sports Illustrated, September 13, 1999)

Newspaper headlines over the past five years have focused on abuses meted out to female athletes and non-athletes. Notable examples of abuses were seen in the O.J. Simpson trial and the media exposure revolving around a Heisman Trophy candidate from the University of Nebraska who attacked and abused his former girlfriend.[1] A more dynamic cases was raised when two former star soccer players from the North Carolina Tar Heels sued their head coach alleging sexual harassment.[2] International headlines greeted a declaration from Boston Bruins hockey player Sheldon Kennedy that he and other young boys were sexually harassed by Graham James, a famous youth hockey coach in Canada.[3] In response to the James incident, the Western Hockey League started requiring criminal background checks for all coaches, managers or league officials.[4] North America is not alone as sexual abuse cases have surfaced throughout the world including Malaysia where a track coach was sent to prison for four years for "outraging the modesty of two young female athletes."[5]

Abuses seen in collegiate and professional sports are also prevalent in youth sports. Millions of young athletes from pee-wee leagues through interscholastic athletics are exposed to possible rape, battery, child abuse, sexual assault and molestation. However, significant steps can be taken

1. Lambe, J. (1996, September 4). "Philips sued for assault ex-girlfriend McEwen says football star often hurt her, once sexually," *The Kansas City Star*, D1.
2. Price, S.L. (1998, December 7). "Anson Dorrance," *Sports Illustrated*, vol. 89, no. 23, pp. 86–103.
3. "Jailed James fearful after aired comments." (1997, January 8). *USA Today*, p. 10C.
4. Id.
5. Abba, R. and Raphael, S. (1996, November 9). "Coach gets jail for molesting athletes," *The New Straits Times*, p. 01

to reduce the chances of sexual abuse in youth sports through the imple-
mentation of a comprehensive sexual abuse prevention program.

Child abuse is a national epidemic affecting over 3 million children in
1994.[6] Approximately 500,000 of these cases involve sexual abuse.[7] In
1992, twelve states reported to the Federal Bureau of Investigation 20,824
forcible rapes of females, of which, 51 percent were juveniles under age 18.[8]

Why the emphasis on youth sports in particular? Whenever there exists
a parental or nurturing environment, children are much more likely to ac-
quiesce to activities they normally would never undertake. Such an environment is the norm between a coach and an athlete. Furthermore, the

---

6. National Committee to Prevent Child Abuse. (1995). *NCPCA Fact Sheet*
[Brochure].

7. Patterson, J. (1995). *Child Abuse Prevention Primer for Your Organization.*
Washington, DC: Nonprofit Risk Management Center.

8. Langan, P.A. & Harlow, C.W. (June, 1994). Child Rape Victims, 1992 Crime
Data Brief. Washington, DC: U.S. Department of Justice. The same data provided an esti-
mate that 17,000 of the 109,062 women raped in 1992 were under age 12.

more the coach is admired and held in awe by the athlete, the more his or her wishes will be followed.[9]

The Law

Criminal sexual abuse cases often revolve around school settings and the special relationship that exists between teachers, coaches, administrators and students. Several states have laws that specifically provide criminal penalties for individuals who use their position of authority or trust to coerce a child into sex.[10] Sexual battery is defined, in part, by Mississippi statute as:

> "(2) A person is guilty of sexual battery if...the person is in a position of trust or authority over the child including without limitation the child's teacher, counselor..., scout leader or coach.[11]"

In Scadden v. State, a high school volleyball coach was convicted of second-degree sexual assault against a volleyball team member.[12] The coach violated Wyoming Statute Section 6-2-30 by using his position of authority to force submission to sexual intercourse.

Civil Liability

Typically, criminal convictions or investigations foster civil litigation. Possibly the most notorious civil suit involving a coach and young ath-

---

9. Eitzen, D.S. (1989). The dark side of coaching and the building of character. In D.S. Eitzen (Ed.), Sports in Contemporary Society (pp. 133). (3rd ed.). New York: St. Martin's Press.

10. States with authority abuse statutes include: New Hampshire (*State v. Collins*, 529 A.2d 945 (N.H. 1987)), Michigan (*People v. Usman*, 406 N.W.2d 824 (Mich. 1987)), and New Mexico (*State v. Gillete*, 699 P.2d 626 (N.M. Ct. App. 1985)). States that have case law creating a duty of individuals in a position of authority include: Alaska (*Skrepich v. State*, 740 P.2d 950 (Alaska Ct. App. 1987) involved a karate teacher who abused his position of authority), North Carolina (*State v. Gilbert*, 385 S.E.2d 815 (N.C. Ct. App. 1989)), Ohio (*State v. Penton*, 588 N.E.2d 951 (Ohio Ct. App. 1990)), and Rhode Island (*State v. Burke*, 522 A.2d 725 (R.I. 1987)).

11. Mississippi Codes, Section 97-3-95 (2) (1972).

12. *Scadden v. State*, 732 P.2d 1036, 1038-1039 (Wyo. 1987).

letes is the Linda Van Housen case.[13] Track coach Michael Ipsen started a sexual relationship with Linda when she was 13-years-old. Two other members of the same running team also claimed to have their first sexual encounters with the coach when they were only 15-years-old. Linda's mother tried to go to the police with the two other victims, but the local police dropped their investigation. Several years after moving out of Ipsen's house and suffering a nervous breakdown, Linda filed a civil suit against Ipsen. The court found Ipsen guilty of sexual abuse of a minor and ordered to pay $1.1 million in damages.

The actual sexual offender is not the only defendant in sexual abuse or assault cases. School districts and sports organizations have been sued for their alleged failure to determine that a volunteer or potential employee had a propensity to engage in sexual misconduct. In Thurmond v. Richmond County Board of Education, the parents of a six-year-old student sued a physical education instructor, and his employer for sexual abuse.[14] After affirming summary judgment for the school, the court noted that there was no evidence of any prior criminal behavior by the teacher. The court also held that the school had successfully screened the teacher through the Georgia Criminal Investigation Center.

Preventing Sexual Assaults

In a study of 197 convicted child molesters released from prison between 1958 and 1974, the recidivism rate for those reconvicted of subsequent sexual crimes was 42 percent.[15] The high likelihood that someone previously convicted of sexual assault crimes might reengage in the same activity requires sport administrators to take steps to weed such individuals from participating in the activity. A criminal history background check provides one method for identifying individuals who are more likely to engage in illegal sexual activity. Nine states currently require coaches or physical education instructors working with schools to be screened for prior criminal convictions.[16] Background checks can be required from both

---

13. Goodman, E. (1993, October). "The coach and his girls, a dangerous bond," *Glamour,* p. 248.

14. *Thurmond v. Richmond County Board of Education,* 428 S.E.2d 392 (Ga. App. 1993).

15. Hanson, R.K., Steffy, R.A. & Gauthier, R. (1993). "Long-term recidivism of child molesters," *Journal of Consulting and Clinical Psychology,* 61, 646-652.

16. Connecticut Gen. Stat. Ann. Section 10-221d(a) (Supp. 1995), Florida State Ann. 231.02 and 231.15 (Supp. 1995), Georgia Code Ann. Section 20-2-211 (Supp. 1995), Nevada Rev. Stat. Ann. Section 391.033 and 391.100 (1991), Ohio Revised Code Ann.

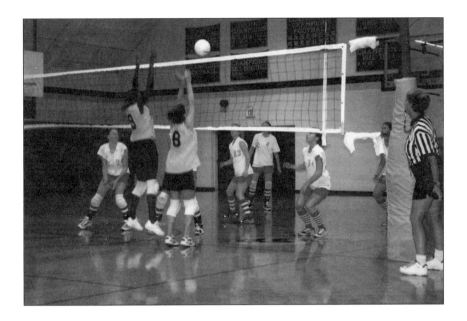

potential employees and volunteers. Such checks can only be conducted after a potential employee or volunteer signs a waiver allowing a background check. Typically, waivers are contained in an employment or volunteer application form. (See attached form.)

Concerns to be addressed when performing background checks include: timeliness of the information, geographic limitations of the information (if a former convict moves between states either during or after parole), the applicant's privacy rights and screening costs (often between $15 and $45 per applicant). Checking backgrounds also requires more than just a criminal history check. Additional screening steps include having in-depth interviews with all references, interviews with current or previous work supervisors and requiring all applicants to read and sign a form agreeing to abide by the organization's sexual abuse policy. Screening should not be limited to just applicants or volunteers. Whenever an overnight activity is scheduled at an individual's house, all individuals residing at the premises should also submit to background checks prior to the event.

Background checks should be coordinated with an organization's comprehensive sexual abuse prevention program. Such a program should focus on the four P's; personnel, program, premises and participants.

Section 3301.541 (Supp. 1994), Oregon Rev. Stat. Section 342.223 (1993), Rhode Island Gen. Laws Section 16-48.1-5 (1988), Tenn. Code Ann. Section 49-5-413 (Supp. 1994), and Washington Rev. Code Section 28A.410.010 (Supp. 1995).

Personnel

In addition to screening and securing qualified personnel, an organization has to make sure everyone involved has adopted the organization's mindset. By carefully drafting precise job descriptions and setting forth what is and is not acceptable conduct, a potential volunteer or employee will know what types of activities are unacceptable. Job descriptions should include the job title, purpose, duties, responsibilities, required qualifications, training and position restrictions. Applicants should be required to sign-off on the application, indicating that they meet all the job description requirements. After thoroughly analyzing the application, the applicant has to be interviewed. Interviewers should be well trained to identify danger areas. For example, many child molesters have limited contact with members of their own peer group.[17] An interviewer can discover this information by asking legally appropriate questions about the applicant's social life.

Every organization should appoint one person as the sexual abuse (and child abuse) resource person who can handle confidential screening material, handle all claims and be a liaison with police and social services professionals. This person could be given a title such as "Special Friend."

Organizations also have to develop specific policies concerning what steps are taken to investigate a sexual abuse claim, how to comfort the abused, who should confront an individual identified as a possible abuser, how to suspend an individual until the allegations are resolved and how to terminate a person's involvement in the organization after being convicted of a sexual offense. The organization has an affirmative obligation to take all appropriate measures to prevent retaliation against the child making a sexual assault claim.

Program

Organizations should schedule a coaches/parent meeting prior to starting each season. This meeting should focus on explaining the organization's sexual abuse prevention program, soliciting assistance from parents to support the program and educating parents on some of the subtle signs of abuse. Parents should also be informed about specific organizational policies. For example, if an organization prohibits overnight activities, parents should know the organization strictly enforces such a rule. Other specific rules should include: prohibiting photographing children except while actively participating in competition, prohibiting one coach from

---

17. Patterson, J. (1994). *Staff Screening Tool Kit*. Washington, DC: Nonprofit Risk Management Center.

taking individual athletes or a team alone on an excursions or overnight trips, having a buddy system in place, only allowing children to ride home with specifically designated drivers and prohibiting coaches, volunteers, officials and visitors from assisting children in removing any clothing; except for sport specific equipment such a football shoulder pads.

Special rules should be adopted concerning specific sports, such as gymnastics, where physical contact is unavoidable. Current gymnastics clothing permits a spotter's hands to slide up a gymnasts body with relative ease. All participants and parents should be informed of the potential for significant bodily contact. Any individuals wishing to avoid such contact can be provided an opportunity to participate in other activities.

Parents should be encouraged to drop-in unannounced to practices or games. Noted sexual abuse researcher Finkelhor and his associates discovered lower rates of abuse in child care programs that encouraged parents to drop in for unannounced visits.[18] Parents should also be allowed access to their children at all times.

Any prohibited conduct needs to be specifically explained to all parties to avoid any confusion, misunderstanding or hurt feelings. A Little League coach in Connecticut claimed he was banned from the league after the parents of an 8-year-old boy complained that the coach gave the kid a congratulatory pat on his backside.[19] The potential confusion concerning what activities are allowed in a given program can lead to difficulty recruiting volunteers. Based on a lack of specific boundaries in some organizations, such as churches, the churches have started having trouble servicing parishioners needs. Clergy members are avoiding counseling parishioners on personal issues for fear of being sued based on a torrent of malpractice claims in that industry.[20] The same concerns facing churches in the 1980s and 1990s is now starting to hit the youth sport industry and should continue for the next decade. Once rules are established and communicated to all parties the incident total should decline.

Premises

The key to protecting premises is access. By limiting facility access an organization can drastically reduce access to children. All facilities should be designed or retrofitted to provide only one entrance and exit. All en-

---

18. Faller, K.C. (1993). *Child Sexual Abuse: Intervention and Treatment Issues*. Washington, DC: U.S. Department of Health and Human Services, National Center on Child Abuse and Neglect.

19. "Coach ousted." (1997, May 2). *USA Today*, p. 1C.

20. Miller, L. (1998, May 8). "Clergy shy away from counseling," *Houston Chronicle*, p. 1D.

trants should be required to sign a guest registry indicating their name and address as well as the reason for attending. If feasible, visitors should be asked for a photo identification card to verify their address. If a facility cannot be designed to eliminate unauthorized access (such as a soccer field in a public park) a designated person should periodically go through the stands and sidelines to monitor the spectators. Additional attention should be given to securing locker rooms, bathrooms, and changing areas. Some programs and schools have designed showers and bathrooms with viewing areas and mounted cameras that can help spot potential abusers, while providing privacy for children using the bathrooms or showers. While cameras can help prove a sexual abuse case, they can also be used inappropriately. Access to cameras or viewing areas should be strictly limited.

Adjacent facilities, including parking lots, might also pose security problems. Inadequate premises lighting is a major concern for night activities. Children should not be allowed to wander in parking lots or wait in public areas without supervision. Parents should be encouraged to pick-up their child directly from the facility or a program volunteer should escort children directly to waiting cars or busses.

Participants

A central component of an organization's sexual assault prevention program is the participant education program. Such a program emphasizes a child's rights and helps them understand that they have a choice. Children should be taught that it is okay to say "No" to some adults. They also should be taught the difference between good and bad touching. Touching should: be in response to the needs of the child, be given with the child's permission, avoid private areas, be open and not secretive and be regulated by the participants age, experience and understanding.[21]

Organizations should develop policies requiring all players to report unapproved or uncomfortable conduct to the "Special Friend" immediately after an incident arises. The "Special Friend" would then take all necessary steps to protect the child, report the incident to appropriate authorities and gather information critical for any future legal needs.

Preventing a potential offender from knowing a child's name can reduce the chances of the offender endearing him or herself to the child. Steps to reduce the chances of identifying participants include: taking names off their uniforms, not publishing lists of player names/addresses, listing parent's work phone numbers-rather than home numbers and cheering teammates on by using their jersey number, rather than their name.

Another major concern which is often overlooked in sexual abuse prevention program entails peer sexual abuse. Numerous cases have been reported alleging hazing type of activities which have involved a sexual abuse element. All such practices need to be prevented. The potential liability for peer on peer sexual assault is immense. Five former cheerleaders sued their school and school district after officials allegedly failed to respond to complaints about constant physical and sexual harassment by football players.[22] In a California case, a student sued a school district for not doing anything to prevent the student from being sexually harassed by her ex-boyfriend. A jury awarded the student $685,000.[23] These cases highlight the need to effectively supervise not just adult contact with children, but child-on-child contact as well, even if such contact occurs outside the event or activity area.

Suggestions for the Future

An organization's sexual abuse prevention program is a good start, but does not address the national problem faced by countless other programs. Therefore, a national campaign involving federal and state authorities along with all youth sports organizations is needed to coordi-

21. Id. at p. 38.
22. Beckett, J. (1996, September 5). "Ex-pep squad members sue.," *The San Francisco Chronicle*, A13.
23. *Hall v. Albany Unified School District* (1999, May). Alameda County Superior Court., *California Bar Journal*, p. 4.

nate various currently existing or planned programs. A coordinated campaign will reduce the chances of a convicted abuser affiliating with different organizations, in different states or different sports. The hallmark of such a campaign could involve a national computer database assessable to all youth organizations. Once an employee or volunteer has successfully completed a criminal background check they could be issued a photograph identification card. The card could be valid for several years. The card could be presented to any sports or youth organization and automatically qualify that individual to work with any youth organization. Only certified individuals would be allowed to work with children.

Conclusion

It is impossible to eliminate the specter of sexual abuse. However, a nonprofit youth sports organization can reduce the chances of facing or losing a sexual abuse suit through utilizing a comprehensive sexual abuse prevention program. Accurate information is critical for any proper screening process. The potential for receiving the most accurate background information can only be accomplished with a national criminal records database available to all qualified nonprofit organizations. While such a system is accessible to law enforcement personnel, a grassroots effort needs to be developed to help filter such information to youth organizations.

After the Facts

Prosecutors dropped a felony charge against a Little League coach accused of molesting a 15-year-old player last year.

Officials with the Forsyth County District Attorney's office said they did not have enough physcial evidence to try Andrew Thomas Harper on one count of taking indecent liberties with a minor.

Kernersville police arrested Harper, 22, of 134 Crestland Drive in June—more than a year after the alleged assault occurred at the house Harper shares with his parents. The teenager spent several nights there after running away and seeking refuge at Harper's house.

"I know it's a big relief for Andy his family and the prople in the program," said Sonny Berry, president of the Kernersville Little League Inc. board of directors. "We would have been amazed if something had come out of this."

Harper could not be reached for comment Tuesday.

Harper stepped down in June after the allegations became public, but he was reinstated several weeks later by Little League officials, who have publicly supported him throughout the summer.

"It was a board decision to allow his to continue," Berry said. "The board didn't want to be the judge and jury."

Harper finished coaching his team last season and began participating in the fall program this month.

The teenager, who was 14 at the time, told a Forsyth County detective about the alleged assault in May of this year. Deputies investigated the case for weeks before turning it over to the police department in Kernersville, where the crime allegedly occurred.

Harper, who works for a building contractor, grew up in Kernersville and participated in Little League until he was old enough to start coaching about four years ago, league officials say (Kumar, 1995).

References

Kumar, Anita. "Coach Back After Charge is Dropped," *Greensboro News and Record*, August 22, 1995.

Nack, William and Don Yaeger. "Every Parent's Nightmare," *Sports Illustrated*, vol. 91, no. 10, September 13, 1999.

Chapter 12

Sports Medicine

The health and welfare of the athlete should be the number one priority in sport.

Todd McLoda

One of the major emphasis in sport today is on the prevention, treatment and rehabilitation of injuries to athletes. On the professional and college level we have made tremendous progress in the medical care that athletes receive on a regular basis. We have team physicians, and trained professional athletic-trainers that supervise every practice and spend countless hours working with our college and pro athletes. Even on the interscholastic level we are beginning to provide better medical care and facilities for our young men and women. Through the development of sports medicine we have learned that an ounce of prevention is worth a pound of cure, that healthy teams win more games, that a minor injury can become worse with improper treatment and that in today's society every injury is a possible lawsuit. With rising health insurance premiums, injuries on any level are expensive, and the prevention and treatment of injuries is becoming a major concern on the Youth Sport level. On the Youth Sport level it is the volunteer coach who has to assume the role of the athletic trainer, and the volunteer coach probably will not have a strong sports medicine background. Dr. Stanley Grosshandler in *Sports Medicine: A Guide for Youth Sports*, developed a series of management guidelines for the Youth Sport coach if and when injuries occur. One of the certainties in sport is that there will be injuries and people who work with young athletes need to be as prepared as possible. Part of the responsibility of a Youth Sport coach in the next millennium is to be able to handle injuries to participants.

Injury Care Responsibilities

Although every youth sport worker should have a basic knowledge of injury care, each team should have one person designated as having primary responsibility for injury care during practices and games. According to Dr. Stanley Grosshandler, a sports medicine expert, this person should assume the following general responsibilities:

1. Become familiar with the medical histories of his players (past injuries, chronic conditions, allergies, etc.) (see Appendix E).
2. Maintain an adequately stocked first aid kit (see Appendix B).
3. Evaluate and give immediate care for injuries.
4. Transport or arrange for transportation of injured players to a medical facility when such a move is deemed necessary.
5. Notify parents of injured players.
6. Determine whether an injured player may safely return to activity (with the assistance of the physician or parents where appropriate) (Hawkins, 1984).

On-the-Field Evaluation

When a player is injured in a game or practice situation, only the person responsible for injury care should go onto the field or court. Several people rushing to the injury scene may result in needless confusion and cause unnecessary concern to the injured player and their parents. The primary concern at this point is to determine if the injury is such that the player should not be moved. In such cases (head and/or neck injury, obvious fracture, etc.) play should be suspended until medical assistance (a physician, emergency medical service, etc.) can be obtained. Fortunately, most injuries are not life-threatening and once a cursory evaluation of the injury has been completed, the player may be moved to the sideline for further evaluation. Based upon the preliminary evaluation, the player may then be:

1. allowed to remain in the game if no further danger from the current injury exists;
2. allowed to return to the game following the completion of further evaluation and/or care if such action removes the probability of further danger from the current injury;
3. withheld from further play pending evaluation of the injury and clearance for return from a physician;
4. transported to a medical facility for further evaluation and care (Hawkins, 1984).

As a college coach I would add two other important elements of an on-the-field evaluation. The first is silence. One of the worst things that can

happen is for the trainer or medical personnel to exclaim how bad the injury is or to make a hasty evaluation. If the injury is serious or looks serious let the doctor or hospital make the call. Too often I have witnessed college athletes panic over an alarming but false evaluation. When an athlete is injured, the less said the better. The second point is that it does not help the injured athlete to have crowds of people standing around. Keep players, fans and parents on the bench or away from the injured athlete if at all possible. The dreaded on-looker-delay is a traffic accident nightmare and one that we do not need when an athlete is injured.

Orthopedic Injuries.

Orthopedic injuries (those involving bones, muscles, tendons, ligaments and joints) are most often of the contusion (bruise), sprain and strain types although fractures and dislocations may occur. The standard recommended procedure for caring for such injuries may be easily remembered by recalling the word "R-I-C-E."

R = Rest
Most injuries respond favorably to rest.

I = Ice
Most orthopedic injuries tend to swell. Since swelling delays
the healing process, ice should be used to slow swelling and

to provide temporary pain relief. Although a common practice, heat should not be used on a recent orthopedic injury since it may actually promote swelling.

C = Compression
Most orthopedic injuries should be wrapped with an elastic wrap to provide pressure and retard swelling.

E = Elevation
Elevating (raising) an injured body part by resting it on a pillow or other elevated surface will also help to reduce the possibility of swelling.

In most cases, the R-I-C-E regimen should be used for the first 24–48 hours following an injury. If swelling persists when this procedure is discontinued, the R-I-C-E plan should be continued (Hawkins, 1984).

Exposed Wounds

Among the most common of all sports-related injuries are abrasions (scrapes), lacerations (cuts) and puncture wounds. The initial concern with open wounds is the control of bleeding, a problem usually found only with deep lacerations. The most effective method of controlling bleeding is the application of pressure directly over the wound using a sterile gauze pad. Once bleeding has been controlled, a second concern is that of infection. Since the threat of infection often poses a more serious danger than the original wound itself, care should be taken to clean all open wounds thoroughly with antiseptic soap and water. Alcohol or hydrogen peroxide may then be used to further cleanse and disinfect the wound. All open wounds should be bandaged using sterile bandage materials. During the healing process, the player may find that a foam pad worn over the bandage will help protect the wound from further damage.

Two special notes should be considered. If there is any question about whether a laceration will require stitches, the player should be referred to a physician for evaluation. Also, because puncture wounds tend to be deep with a small external opening, there exists a chance of a foreign body being imbedded in the wound. Therefore, it is recommended that all puncture wounds be referred to a physician (Hawkins, 1984).

Heat Illness

In those areas of the country where temperature and humidity tend to become very high (90 degrees + 80% + respectively), heat illness is a threat to the well-being of the young athlete. The most common form of heat illness is muscle cramps, usually occurring in the calves. These may be effectively reduced by applying a steady, firm grasp to the cramping muscle or be gently kneading the muscle. Once the cramp has subsided, gentle stretching may be used. Also, since cramps are heat-related, the athlete should be given fluids (water, electrolyte drink, etc.) to replace lost body fluids.

Heat exhaustion is a serious form of heat illness in which the body temperature may become quite high. The player will continue to perspire and may complain of headache, dizziness, nausea and/or vomiting. Any player experiencing such symptoms on a hot day should be rapidly cooled by removing excess clothing, fanning and/or sponging with cool, water-soaked towels.

Heat stroke is the most serious form of heat illness and may be potentially fatal. Therefore, its symptoms must be quickly recognized and appropriate actions taken. The player suffering from heat stroke will usually have a temperature of 104 degrees or more and will have hot, dry skin. The player may develop seizures and lapse into a coma. He must be rapidly cooled.

Victims of both heat exhaustion and heat stroke should be taken immediately to a medical facility for treatment and should be given fluids, usually by the intravenous route. Also, while it is true that heat illness is often accompanied by a loss of sodium from the body, salt tablet should never be used in the prevention or care of heat illness unless specifically ordered by a physician (Hawkins, 1984).

As a former high school and college coach let me say that restraint needs to be exercised during warm weather. There is a fine line between conditioning and abuse of athletes. It is an easy line to cross, because I did so on a few occasions and I knew better, but I let the emotion of the moment replace common sense. No pain, no gain in my opinion may be one of the worst slogans ever used in sport, because it is untrue and forces many youngsters out of participation. Sports should be about fun and excitement not pain and suffering. The days of withholding water either as punishment or as a way to make athletes tougher is over. Heat exhaustion and heat stroke are both serious and both can be prevented. The Youth Sport coach needs to be alert to both conditions and to use common sense and good judgment during warm weather practices and games.

Cardiopulmonary Resuscitation (CPR)

The goal of CPR is to provide oxygen quickly to the brain, heart and other vital organs until appropriate definitive medical treatment can restore normal heart and pulmonary functions (Thomas, 1993).

In December of 1997, I traveled to Montgomery County, North Carolina to watch my daughter, Elizabeth, cheer for her High School basket-

ball team. My daughter's school was playing against an old friend, Bobby Martin, who 17 years before had been my assistant when I was a rookie head football coach on the high school level. Bobby and I had both changed schools several times, but we had always managed to keep in touch. Now on a cold winter evening I was traveling the back roads of rural North Carolina to watch my daughter cheer and see an old friend coach. The game was a blow out for Coach Martin and his team was winning easily as the clock wound down. With about 20 seconds left in the game I noticed a small commotion on the home team's bench, and I watched Bobby collapse. The assistant coach ran to the scorer's table to try and stop the game. The horn sounded and the game ended in a state of confusion as players, parents and fans came out on to the court. Someone went to the Principal's office to call the rescue squad, and an administrator attempted to clear the gym. I sat on the bleachers and watched as they laid Coach Martin on the floor near his bench. No one seemed to know what to do as Bobby laid on the floor. Finally after several minutes of confusion, the coach of the other team began administering CPR to the unconscious Bobby Martin. For approximately 15 minutes, the other coach continued his CPR efforts until the rescue squad arrived, which was 20 minutes after Coach Martin had initially collapsed. I watched as members of the rescue squad hit Bobby Martin three times with an electric shock, and I saw his body jolted by the electricity. Finally 30 minutes after the game had ended, Coach Martin was placed on a stretcher and transported to Montgomery County Hospital where he was pronounced dead.

In the previous September during a football game at the University of North Carolina, Jim Knight, a member of the officiating crew collapsed on the field with a heart attack. However, because of the UNC Sports Medicine Staff, the rescue squad personnel on duty and the available equipment, Jim Knight is alive today. In fact, several medical experts felt that Knight was lucky to be where he was and that his heart attack almost certainly would have been fatal anywhere else. An Atlantic Coast Conference football official suffers a heart attack and lives to referee again, a high school basketball coach dies and leaves behind an unfulfilled legacy.

As a college assistant football coach for 14 years we always had trainers at practice and games, so I did not have to worry about knowing first aid and CPR. However, few Youth Sport coaches have or will have the same luxury. It is important that Youth Sport coaches have training in CPR, and have a basic understanding of first aid and what to do in case of a medical emergency. When the emergency happens it is too late then to plan what steps to take, planning needs to be done beforehand, and emergency procedures need to be practiced. Just like we practice fire drills in the public schools, Youth Sport coaches need to have an emergency action plan, and they need to practice what to do.

I tell the tragedy of Bobby Martin because I will always believe that a proper medical response could have saved his life. As a Youth Sport coach, official or administrator, take the time to learn CPR and some basic first aid.

Diseases

Many children are denied the opportunity to participate in sports because of the existence of disease. While it is recommended that a child not exercise vigorously when she is ill, especially if a fever is involved, many chronic diseases such as diabetes and some types of asthma may respond quite favorably to exercise. Many other conditions may also allow for normal sports participation without undue risk to the child. There have been numerous successful professional athletes who have had diabetes, asthma, sickle cell trait, or anemia, convulsive disorders and many other such diseases. The family physician should be consulted prior to making a decision about sports participation based upon the existence of disease (Hawkins, 1984).

Common Injuries

Two other common injuries that we sometimes see on the Youth Sport level are fainting and nose bleeds.

Due to any one of a number of causes, including excitement, a player may simply faint. When a player faints, he should be allowed to remain lying down with the feet slightly elevated to increase blood flow to the brain. If breathing and pulse are normal, the player should regain consciousness spontaneously. This process should not be hastened by shaking or slapping the child or pouring water on the face. Simply calling the child's name while remaining calm will usually do the trick. If consciousness does not return, medical assistance should be sought.

One of the most common injuries, especially in contact sports, is the nose bleed. Nose bleeds may result from a blow to the nose, in which case the possibility of nasal fracture must be considered, or the nose may simply begin to bleed without apparent cause. In either case, the player should be placed in a sitting position and pressure applied to the side of the nose to close the nostril. In most cases, bleeding will cease within five minutes. If bleeding persists and is unable to be controlled, the player should be taken to a medical facility (Hawkins, 1984).

"Red Flag" Emergencies

The following conditions should be considered "red flag" emergencies and should be referred immediately to professional medical personnel for care:

1. absence of breathing (establish an open airway and initiate rescue breathing or CPR),
2. absence of pulse (initiate CPR),
3. unconsciousness with inability to arouse,
4. convulsions,
5. excessive bleeding,
6. severe head and/or neck pain, especially with dizziness, nausea or vomiting,
7. difficulty breathing or significant wheezing,
8. heat stroke and heat exhaustion (Hawkins, 1984).

Injuries are going to happen in sport, they are part of the game. It is the responsibility of the coach to be prepared to handle injuries as they occur, but to also practice preventive medicine. The Youth Sport coach not only may have to drive the van, line the field, coach the team, but be the athletic trainer as well.

The following recommendations can help prevent situations that may lead to injuries and subsequent litigation:

1. Require a physical examination before the participant engages in the sport (see Appendix E).
2. Make certain all equipment fits properly.
3. Inspect equipment for defects and facilities for hazards (see Appendix I).
4. Obtain medical insurance coverage for the youth sport participant and liability insurance for the coach and physician (see Appendix F).
5. Adopt a medical plan for emergency treatment (see Appendix D).
6. Assign activities within the participant's range of ability and commensurate with his/her size, skill and physical condition.
7. Prepare the participant gradually for all physical drills and progress from the simple to complex tasks.
8. Warn the participant of all possible dangers inherent in the sport (see Appendix H).
9. Adopt a policy regarding injuries. Do not attempt to be a "medical specialist" in judging the physical condition of the participant under your care.
10. Require a physician's medical permission before permitting seriously ill or injured participants to return to normal practice.
11. Avoid moving the injured participant until it is safe to do so.
12. Conduct periodic medical in-service training programs for all volunteer coaches (Hawkins, 1984).

After the Facts

As children, they ran and jumped freely without concern for the minor scrapes and bumps that mom and dad patched up with Band-Aids.

Now, as teens, they are competing intensely in high school and college sports, an arena where sports medicine specialists say the young athlete is frequently sustaining more serious injuries that can shatter dreams of future careers.

The specialists said increased incidents of what they call "overuse injuries" result in cases of tendinitis, bursitis and stress fractures due to longer sports seasons, intensive training camps and the tendency of teens to play several sports year-round without giving the body a rest.

Dr. Josesph Feinberg, clinical chief of sports medicine at Kessler Institute in West Orange, attributes the injuries to a greater desire to

compete on a higher level where there is prestige and eventually money involved.

"I just think that puts an increasing demand on the athlete," he said.

Dr. Ira Shapiro, a chiropractic sports physician in Old Bridge, said young athletes injure themselves through overtraining in an attempt to improve their performance.

"Athletic improvement only happens when you push the body," Shapiro said.

Shapiro, who also is a consulting chiropractor for athletic teams in the Old Bridge public schools, said athletes are engaging in much more demanding workouts, striving to do that little bit extra that could prove to be the edge in a record-setting performance.

"There's a fine line between work and overwork," Sahpiro said. "The average athlete can sustain all-out body stress two to three times a week."

Feinberg, Sahpiro and other sports medicine specialists also have attributed the rise in injuries among young athletes to longer school sports seasons, intensive sports camps and participation in several sports year round.

Shapiro said he tells young athletes that the most highly conditioned body has a limit at which it can perform.

Athletes, on any level, have to give their bodies time to rest or injuries will occur, he added.

While sports medicine specialists agree the injuries usually respond well to rest, they note there is often self-imposed or external pressure to resume sports activity too soon.

All athletes, including young ones, should heed certain warning signs when they feel something is wrong. For example, he said they should be concerned if there is "localized pain in the joint, some stiffness with slight loss in range of movement" or no improvement after a period of rest.

"These symptoms should alert an athlete that an injury is on the way," he said.

Feinberg, like other experts, noted that with medical and technical advancements, injuries that in the past might have been ignored are now being detected through more advanced technology and can be treated before becoming serious problems.

Feinberg, who also is a team physician for Newark Academy, St. Peter's College and Montclair State College, said the key to treating injuries when they occur is being seen by a sports physician before they get worse.

"That's a very important thing," Feinberg said. "If you see it early on, you can change things."

Dr. Richard Braver, of the Foot-Wise Podiatry & Sports Medicine Center in Englewood, agreed, noting prompt attention to overuse injuries can reduce pain and the chances of long-term damage. He urges parents to seek medical consultation for their children when they notice young athletes limping or showing distress in their limbs.

He added repetitive movements that exceed the tolerance of muscles or joints lead to stress fractures, Achilles tendmitis, shin splints and plantar fascitis.

Although ankle sprains remain the most common scholastic sports injury, medical experts said there is an increasing frequency in overuse injuries that, left untreated, result in bursitis, tendinitis and stress fractures.

"When we at Kessler see a problem, we address other related factors," Feinberg said, referring to examining other parts of the body near the injury as a way of preventing other problems.

For instance, he said, if a pitcher injures his shoulder, therapists at Kessler will examine the back and neck area as well as the throwing motion of the pitcher, trying to detect whether other body parts may be affected.

While Kessler is mostly known for rehabilitation of serious injuries and severe joint diseases, the institution also provides care for high school and college athletes and the weekend warrior as well.

There are certain basics, and Feinberg stressed that more attention should be given toward conditioning so an athlete has a year-round program that incorporates rest while allowing him or her to stay in shape.

At Kessler, Feinberg said, an injured athlete receives therapy that involves some type of exercise.

But then there are some injuries that have little to do with conditioning. Sports medicine specialists note that the quality of the equipment is not always up to par with the demands.

As soccer has increased in popularity to rival football, doctors say each fall they treat an epidemic of heel pain caused by tendinitis. They attribute the phenomenon to poorly designed shoes, adding the design of soccer shoes has not caught up with the rest of the sports shoe industry (Carter, 1993).

References

Appenzeller, Herb. *Risk Management in Sport*. Carolina Academic Press, Durham, North Carolina, 1998.

Appenzeller, Herb and Guy Lewis. *Youth Sports*. Greensboro Printing Company, Greensboro, North Carolina, 1981.

Carter, Barry. "The Body has a Limit at Which it can Perform," Newark Star-Ledger, January 24, 1993.

Hawkins, Jerald. *Sports Medicine: A Guide for Youth Sports*. Carolina Marketing Associates, Inc., Greensboro, North Carolina, 1984.

Roy, Steven and Richard Irvin. *Sports Medicine*. Prentice-Hall, Inc., Englewood Cliffs, New Jersey, 1983.

Thomas, Clayton L. *Taber's Cyclopedic Medical Dictionary*. F.A. Davis Company, Philadelphia, Pennsylvania, 1993.

Chapter 13

Observations and Recommendations

There is no knowledge that is not power.
Ralph Waldo Emerson

Youth Sport has become a vital part of the fabric of the American society. As we enter a new millennium, the opportunities for children to participate in adult organized and directed sporting experience will continue to increase. In the 1950s and 1960s there was Little League baseball, and if a person lived near a city, there might be Pop Warner football or a YMCA. Opportunities to play organized sports were limited for many children. If a young person wanted to play on an organized team, the only real opportunity was at the local high school. That is not true today. The 1970s and 1980s, witnessed the growth of non-school sponsored athletic teams, such as AAU basketball, select soccer, elite softball, All-Star gymnastics and cheerleading squads. Today's young athlete may play for his/her school team and one or more youth sport teams at the same time. It is not uncommon for today's student to play two or three school sponsored games during the week and then travel and play in local, state or regional youth sport tournaments on the weekend. Some student athletes have even abandoned their high school teams for Select and Elite squads that practice, play and travel year round. A softball coach recently stated that she no longer recruited players off of high school teams, she looked for players on the summer travel squads, because that was where the better players were. Some experts have even predicted that high school sports will disappear by the midpoint of the next century to be replaced by the Youth Sport model. As we see more and more children finding their competitive sporting experience outside the traditional educational setting, it is critical that we educate the thousands of volunteers that provide the leadership in Youth Sport. This book has been written to serve as an educational tool for all who provide the Youth Sport experience. The goal of this publication has been to make volunteers and professionals aware of the legal ramifications of providing a sport experience today for children and young adults. Our society is one that has and will continue to use state and fed-

eral courts to address real or imagined aggrieved wrongs. The benefit of litigation is that lawsuits produce information, and this information can be
used to make sport safer and a better experience for the participants. We
have seen lawsuits on the professional, collegiate and interscholastic level
and now we are seeing more litigation on the Youth Sport level. The lawsuits on the Youth Sport level reveal that good intentions are not enough
anymore when it comes to the health and welfare of children. *In loco parentis* now extends from the classroom to the Little League park, swimming pool, gymnastics club or anywhere else children are organized into
teams. The volunteer coach, official and administrator can be held to the
same standards and levels of conduct as the professional, collegiate or interscholastic counterpart. Lack of salary, ignorance or limited experience
is no longer a valid excuse for negligence by people in a leadership position. The volunteer, the parent or grandparent who just wants to help out
or who is pressured into coaching, has to be aware of the legal obligations
and responsibilities that leadership creates. A few years ago many coaches
would not allow athletes to drink water during practice because of the
mistaken belief that water would make a player sick. Times have changed,
and that old idea about water is obsolete, and paid coaches and administrators know that and have changed the rules for practice and games. Most
of the new information we have about sport has come because of litigation
where a tragedy occurred. Lawsuits have forced coaches, officials and administrators to alter or change the rules of the game. Coaches and administrators on the college and high school level understand the threat of
being sued, and this threat has in many instances helped create a better
and safer sporting experience. It appears we are going to continue to see
more and more litigation in sport on every level, but especially the youth
sport level. From injuries and accidents, to gender equity, to accommo-
dating individuals with disabilities and sexual abuse, Youth Sport is a
whole new legal ball game. The knowledge is out there to create a better
sport experience, the challenge is to educate and inform the volunteers
who manage Youth Sport.

   Let me conclude by offering 10 recommendations for Youth Sport leaders that can help to provide a better and safer experience for children in
sport.

1. Always put the safety and welfare of the participant first.

This is the simplest and most common sense guideline and yet it may be
the most difficult to follow. In the heat of competition, playing in the big
game, championship on the line, parents, coaches, and administrators

sometimes get carried away. Short term goals and rewards often replace long range values and beliefs. Youth Sport is a game for children, not the Super Bowl, and the excitement of the moment should never replace the reality of the consequences. Do not rush to judgment when it concerns the health and safety of children.

2. Warn participants about dangers and the inherent risk of the activity.

The mother who warns her child about the dangers of touching a hot stove does not always guarantee that the child will never touch a hot stove and get burned. However it is important to warn children about certain inherent risk, because in certain situations it may prevent an unnecessary injury. Exactly how does a coach or administrator warn children is not clear. It is important that children be told what the risks are for a certain activity.

3. Teach proper technique and correct skills.

In every sport, there is a right way to do something and a wrong way. The correct way is usually the safest and will help to eliminate certain unnecessary accidents. Techniques have changed over the years, and most of the changes have made sport safer. Teaching a baseball player to run over the catcher, or even to jump over the catcher used to be correct, but not today. The coach needs to be as up to date as possible when teaching children how to do something. Clinics, colleges and camps are all places where coaches can go to learn correct techniques, and how to teach the needed skills of the sport. Just as yesterdays meal will not satisfy today's hunger, the old way of doing something may no longer be appropriate. Coaching is teaching and teaching is a life long process of learning.

4. Explain and demonstrate safety rules.

Sports rules today serve the purpose of making the activity safer and better. Coaches need to be certain that players know the rules and why they exist. A football player that knows about spearing and knows what can happen should be less likely to spear someone in a game or practice. Posters about why to wear a helmet in baseball, or a mouth piece in football can be very useful. Ignorance of the rules by coaches and players is no longer acceptable.

5. Check facilities on a regular basis.

Unsafe facilities are a leading cause of injuries and accidents on every level. The coach and administrator has an obligation to inspect facilities on a regular basis, and if necessary postpone or cancel an activity. Wet floors, unsafe backstops, holes in the playing surface, are just a few examples of unsafe playing conditions. Look for potential hazards in order to prevent unnecessary accidents.

6. Inspect equipment on a regular basis.

Football helmets, catchers equipment, gymnastic mats are all examples of equipment that needs to be checked. All equipment should be fitted properly, certified and worn correctly. Using out-dated, hand-me-down, used equipment is not a good idea anymore. Good equipment, fitted properly, worn correctly, and well-maintained is critical for today's athlete.

7. Post warning signs in facilities explaining dangerous areas and proper behavior.

A picture is worth a thousand words and the administrator and coach wants to make sure athletes get the picture. Swimming pools, gymnastic equipment, locker rooms all have the potential to cause injuries. It is very important that children see examples of proper behavior, and that improper behavior is not tolerated. Children are most susceptible to injuries and accidents when they are doing things they should not be doing. Running in a pool area is dangerous behavior and is an example of something that cannot be allowed. Post warning signs and then enforce proper behavior.

8. Always supervise activities.

Young people need supervision, that is one reason parents want their child involved in Youth Sport. A coach or administrator becomes the *in loco parentis*, becomes that parent, and should supervise children accordingly. It is when the coach is not present that children tend to get out of hand, and injuries occur. Always supervise, and the younger the child and the more dangerous the activity, the more specific the supervision has to be.

9. Develop a plan in case of an emergency.

Schools have fire drills, to prepare for an emergency, because it is a lack of preparation that causes additional injuries. The coach and administrator need to prepare and develop a plan to deal with serious injuries, because most youth league teams will not have a team doctor or an athletic trainer. We have made great strides in sport medicine over the last few years, but medical personnel are just beginning to be found on the high school level. On the Youth Sport level the coach is the trainer, and first aid and the CPR training become critical. Know what to do beforehand, do not just wish something else had been done afterwards.

10. Never assume anything with children, be prepared for the unexpected, anticipate problems.

One of the rules of leadership is to never assume anything and with children that is a good policy. Children by their very age have a lack of experience and what is standard knowledge for an adult, might be a lesson not yet learned by a child. The innocence of youth may be caused by an ignorance of the possible dangers of an activity and it is the adult that serves as the protector. Remember that children and adults do not have the same frame of reference, and never will. Be prepared for everything and anticipate problems.

Years ago the Little League coach would usually hear the words, thanks for being a volunteer. Today that same coach is just as likely to hear, I am going to sue. We have a changing sports climate in the United States, but the bottom line is that we need to make sport participation as safe, as fair and as much fun for our children as possible. Remember that today's youth are the future, let us protect and nurture that future.

After the Facts

Oh to be 11 and playing baseball in the late-afternoon sunshine at Charlotte's Randolph Park.

As rush-hour commuters head home on nearby Randolph Road, Gammon Hall is running bases with his First Charlotte Bank team in the Myers Park Trinity League.

Let the weary 5 o'clock driver watch the bumper in front of him, just so long as Gammon can giddily watch coach Tom Cox and the hot-air balloon lazing past overhead.

"Position. Feet. Knees. Good," Cox instructs his 11 young pupils in the science of hitting. "Take a cut."

"I get to come out here and do what I do best," said Gammon, a first baseman/pitcher and Eastover Elementary fifth-grader who has played ball nearly half his 11 years. "I'm having a good time. I'm having a great time."

What a world this would be if youth baseball was sunshine, hot-air balloons and kids getting to do what they do best.

But as The Great American Pastime, kiddie style, revs up this week throughout the Carolinas, reality is about to come sliding into home with spikes flashing dangerously.

From screaming coaches who think they're the second coming of Billy Martin to obsessed parents who confuse Junior for Jose Canseco, the obnoxious minority is about to turn dreams of the young into nightmares for all ages.

So before the volunteer umpire shrieks "Play ball!" you'd better reach for the Rolaids and earplugs. Or better yet, shriek "Chill out!" to the losers on the sidelines while you scream "You're the greatest" to the young winners on the field.

"We have so many parents who live their lives through their children's activities," said Mecklenburg County recreation official Isaac Applewhite, who holds clinics for youth coaches.

"Parents," said Jim Austin of the York (S.C.) Recreation Department, "are necessary evils in youth sport."

From Little League baseball to the Sardis Angels T-ball team in Charlotte, sanity generally prevails.

"We feel participation is the key," said Steve Weller from Little League headquarters in Williamsport, Pa. "We stress the family. The little guy is playing ball, his dad's coaching and his mom's in the concession stand. The real priority is to enjoy the game for what it is."

On the Angels, where the 6- and 7-year-olds hit off a tee, everyone gets to play the infield if they want.

"Everyone's going to get caught up in it once in a while," said Angels skipper Paul Bailey, a mechanical engineer at Duke Power Co. "But in T-ball, people have a grasp on reality. With a 6-year-old, no telling what they'll do."

"We cheer and yell and whistle and have a good old time," said Debbie Stovall, whose two sons play in the Trinity League division for 10- to 12-year-olds. "But nobody screams at the umps."

Make that nearly nobody.

For every 10 enlightened parents and coaches, there's going to be a few who holler at the umpires, pressure the children and ruin it for everyone.

Where's the joy when your positive cheers are drowned out by the whines of a domineering parent or coach? Gone the way of stadium grass and inexpensive ballpark hotdogs.

It doesn't have to be that way. Persuade every last mom, dad and coach to appreciate

the sunshine and hot-air balloons as much as their kids. If we do that, we can craft a game worth shouting about.

And a game every bit as sweet as the millions of children who adore it.

"I have this picture from my all-star days," Weller said of the framed photo he keeps in his office. "It has my mom, dad, brother, sister, aunt and uncle. As long as I live, they'll be in that picture. That's how I remember Little League baseball."

"Let them play," said Applewhite, who preaches the point at coaches' clinics. "Let them have their time. It's America's sport. It's the sport of champions."

"Remove yourself from shouting and screaming at your child. They don't need that. Turn your love on. Just cheer and say, 'Yah'" (Garfield, 1990).

References

Garfield, Ken. "Angry Adults Needn't Ruin Kids Baseball," *The Charlotte Observer*, March 23, 1990.

Appendices

A. Employee/Volunteer Application Form
    Copyright: Gil Fried, University of New Haven, 1999

B. Athletic Training Kit Checklist
    Copyright: Bob Casmus, Catawba College, 1999

C. Sample Accident/Injury Report
    Copyright: Herb Appenzeller, Managing Sports, 1993

D. Emergency Contact Information
    Copyright: Jim Hand, Wingate University, 1999

E. Parent's Insurance Authorization
    Copyright: Herb Appenzeller, Managing Sports, 1993

F. Parental Medical Consent Form
    Copyright: Todd McLoda, Wingate University, 1999

G. Statement of Risk
    Copyright: Todd McLoda, Wingate University, 1999

H. Sample Equipment and Facility Inspection Checklist
    Copyright: Herb Appenzeller, Managing Sports, 1993

Appendix A

EMPLOYEE/VOLUNTEER APPLICATION FORM

Full legal name: _____

Prior names or aliases: _____

Complete address:_____

Home and work numbers: (___) _____ (___) _____

Social security number: _____

Driver's license number, state and expiration date:_____
    (only for volunteers)

Date of birth: _____(only for volunteers)

List all coaching certificates or diplomas: _____
_____

List all prior involvement in youth athletics:_____
_____

List three personal and business references including current phone numbers:

Personal (1) _____
           _____

           (2) _____
           _____

           (3) _____
           _____

Business (1) _____
           _____

           (2) _____
           _____

           (3) _____
           _____

List all prior residences in the past ten years: _____
_____

Have you ever been convicted of any felony, in any state
or country:_____

If yes, please describe the felony committed and your current legal status (parole, probation, etc.): _____

I understand and agree that:

1) It is the policy of this organization to deny employment or volunteer opportunities for individuals who have been convicted of any violent crime or any crime against any person(s).

2) This organization has a strict confidentiality and appeals process concerning the handling the applications of individuals with prior criminal histories.

1) This application is valid for two years and a new application has to be completed immediately thereafter.

2) By submitting this application I, the applicant, affirm that all the foregoing information I have provided is true and correct.

3) By submitting this application I, the applicant, agree (in return for being allowed to work/volunteer) that if any of the foregoing information is incorrect, I will forever indemnify and hold this youth organization harmless for any acts or omissions on my behalf solely as it relates to the incorrect information I have provided.

4) By submitting this application I, the applicant, voluntarily waive my privacy rights only to the extent necessary for the youth organization to verify the foregoing information through any reasonable means, including, but not limited to criminal background check(s).

Printed Name:_____
Signature: _____
Date: _____

Appendix B

Summer Camp/Recreation Team
ATHLETIC TRAINING KIT CHECK-LIST
(copyright 1999 by Bob Casmus, Catawba College)

EMERGENCY MATERIALS

BP Cuff
Stethoscope
Pen Light
Thermometer-Oral/5 Steri
   Temp pkgs
3–5 Bee Sting Swabs (outdoor sports)

OINTMENTS

Vaseline or Skin Lube (tube/jar)
Triple Antibiotic oint. (1 tube or 5 pkgs)
Analgesic Balm

LIQUIDS/SUSPENSIONS

Eye Irrigating Solution
Saline irrigating rinse
Alcohol
Hydrogen Peroxide
Isoquin/Germicidal Solution

TAPE SUPPLIES

Heel & Lace Pads
1/2" white tape – 1 roll
1" white tape – 2 rolls
1 1/2" white tape – 4 rolls

BANDAGES/BANDAIDS

Eye Pad
Nose Plugs – 5
1" Bandaid Strips – 10
Telfa Pads – 5
Sterile Gauze Pads – 10
3" Sterile Gauze Roll – 2
3" Non-Sterile Gauze Roll – 2
4" Ace Bandage – 2

6" Ace Bandage – 2
4" or 6" Double Length Ace
   Bandage – 1
Steri-Strips – 2 pkgs (1/4" x 1/8")
Large Bandaids

OTHER

Tongue Blades – 10
Cotton Tip Applicators – 10
Scissors – 1
Nail Clippers – 1
Small note pad & pen
Alcohol Wipes – 5
Slings – 2 (different sizes)
Finger Aluma-Splint – 1
Felt/Foam
2 Quarters
Pen & Paper
Plastic Bags – 10
Brown Paper Bags – 1
Rubber Gloves – 3 pair
Sugar Packets – 3
Bio-Hazard Pack/Personal Protection
   Pack
Emergency Cards of Participants

SPRAYS

Tape Adherent

*note or place in kit those athletes who
   have asthma inhalers or Epi-Pens!

** list health care facilities and phone
   numbers in kit

Appendix C

Sample Accident/Injury Report

I. (1) Athlete's Name: _____
    (2) Sport engaged in at time of injury: _____
    (3) Position: _____
    (4) Date of Injury: _____
    (5) When did the injury occur
        (i.e., practice, game, other): _____

II. (1) Location of injury:
    Head _____   Arm _____   Foot _____
    Neck _____   Shoulder _____ Eye _____
    Back _____   Leg _____   Chest _____
    Face _____   Hand _____   Finger _____

III. (1) Describe treatment rendered for this injury: _____
     _____
     (2) List person(s) who administered treatment (i.e., specific
         trainers or physicians, or other staff members: _____
     _____
     (3) Did the athlete refuse treatment? ____ Yes ____ No
     (4) Describe any and all follow-up treatments: _____
     _____
     (5) Was the athlete hospitalized for this injury? ____ Yes ____ No
     (6) If yes, state name of hospital and nature of treatment:_____
     _____
     (7) Indicate practices missed: _____
     (8) Indicate games missed: _____

Report prepared by:_____
Title:_____
Date report prepared: _____

Appendix D

Emergency Contact Information

Student's Name: _____

Address: _____

_____

Telephone Number: _____

Age: _____Birth Date: _____

Emergency Contact (Name and phone numbers)

1) _____
            (Name)   (Relationship)

_____
     (Home Telephone)   (Business Telephone)

2) _____
            (Name)   (Relationship)

_____
     (Home Telephone)   (Business Telephone)

Presently under the following medication:_____

_____

Presently allergic to the following medication: _____

_____

Presently wear contact lenses? _____

Presently wear glasses?_____

Presently a diabetic, hemophiliac or have hearing problems?

If so, please state: _____

_____

Appendix E

Insurance Information Form

Parents Complete and Return To:

Name of Athlete: _____   Sport:_____

Home Address:_____   Phone: _____

Father/Guardian: _____   Mother/Guardian: _____

Address:_____   Address: _____

_____   _____

Phone: Home-   Work-   Phone: Home-   Work-

Medical Ins. Co. _____   Medical Ins. Co._____

_____   _____

Address:_____   Address: _____

Ins. Co. Phone: _____   Ins. Co. Phone: _____

Policy No. _____   Policy No._____

Is the company or plan listed considered a Health Maintenance Organization (HMO) or a Preferred Provider Organization (PPO)?

Yes_____   No_____

Appendix F

Parental Medical Consent Form

I hereby grant permission to the _____ (name of institution) and their duly authorized representatives, to consent to first aid, emergency medical care and all other medical or surgical care them deem reasonably necessary to the health and well being of my son or daughter.

Also, when necessary for executing such care, I grant permission for hospitalization at an accredited hospital.

_____
Student's Name

_____
Parent or Guardian's Signature

_____
Date

Appendix G

Statement of Risk

While the benefits derived from athletic participation are great, there are also calculated risks involved in such competition. Participants and parents/guardians are hereby advised that an element of risk is present that could result in injury, total paralysis or death in all such participation.

As parent or legal guardian of _____, I hereby give my consent for his/her practice of play in athletic events and understand the inherent risks involved in such participation.

_____   _____
Signature of Parent/Legal Guardian (or spouse)   Date

I, _____, understand the inherent risks involved in any athletic participation and accept that my participation could result in injury, paralysis or death.

_____   _____
Signature of Athlete   Date

Appendix H

Sample Equipment and Facility Inspection Checklist
Outdoor Playing Fields Checklist
(i.e., Football, Soccer, Lacrosse, etc.)

Area   Condition/Remarks

(1) Field surface condition
(2) Uncovered drains:
(3) Drainage of field:
(4) Presence of unrelated equipment on field:
(5) Debris: Condition of benches and bleachers:
(6) Condition of goals:
(7) Adequate lighting:
(8) Boundaries marked between playing areas:

Date of inspection: _____

Time of inspection: _____

Recommendations: _____

Name of Inspector: _____

Signature of Inspector: _____

Baseball/Softball Field

Area   Condition/Remarks

 (1) Infield/Basepaths/Mound:
 (2) Outfield:
 (3) Batting circle:
 (4) On-Deck area:
 (5) Warning track:
 (6) Backstop-screening:
 (7) Sidelines:
 (8) Drainage of field:
 (9) Uncovered drains:
(10) Lighting
(11) Debris:
(12) Presence of unrelated equipment on field:
(13) Benches and bleachers:

Date of inspection: _____
Time of inspection: _____
Recommendations: _____
                     _____
                     _____
                     _____

Name of inspector: _____
Signature of inspector: _____

Table of Cases

About the Author

My organized youth sport experience goes back to the summer of 1960 when I went to visit my grandparents in Marshville, North Carolina. The recreation department sponsored a Little League team and I was invited to participate. I was a nine-year-old right fielder playing on a dirt outfield constantly praying that no one would hit the ball to me. My coach, who was a college student home for summer vacation, gave me very specific batting instructions. I was not to swing the bat under any circumstances. My job was to go up to the plate, squat down, and get a walk. I remember being scared to death of one of the opposing pitchers, a hard-throwing, slightly wild, huge, 12 year old monster. I never took a swing that entire season, but I did walk several times to get on base. In spite of a less than stellar beginning, I went on to play three seasons of Little League baseball back home in Greensboro, North Carolina, one year of Pop Warner football, and several seasons of YMCA and summer league basketball.

In the fall of 1969 I enrolled at Presbyterian College in Clinton, South Carolina with the hope of one day playing college football. The Athletic Director and Head Football Coach Cally Gault, however, took one look at me and offered me an athletic scholarship not to play. So for four years I served as the Sports Information Director for the Presbyterian College Blue Hose. I did have the opportunity to practice and travel with the men's basketball team for two years, but it was my experience off campus for the last two years of college that served as the foundation of this book. For two years every afternoon a friend, Claude Underwood, and myself ran an after-school sports program for the Clinton YMCA. There was no building, so in the fall and spring we played on a vacant lot across from the high school and in the winter we moved to the National Guard Armory. Claude and I conducted practices, divided up teams, coached, refereed, and sometimes played all at the same time. We went from 3:00 to 5:00, four days a week. We played football and practiced for the punt, pass, and kick competition in the fall, basketball during the winter, and baseball and softball in the spring. There were no uniforms, scoreboards, bleachers, or parents, but everybody played and everybody had fun. Several of our elementary school age boys went on to become good high school athletes.

After teaching and coaching on the interscholastic level in North Carolina and completing a Masters Degree in History Education from the University of North Carolina at Greensboro (UNC-G) and a Masters in Sport Management from the University of Massachusetts, I began to come in contact with some negative aspects of Youth Sport. When I began my Doctoral Studies at UNC-G in Physical Education in 1982 I knew that I wanted to concentrate my research in the area of Youth Sport.

Now as a parent, my children have participated in t-ball, baseball, softball, gymnastics, martial arts, basketball, and soccer on the youth sport level. In addition, I have served as an umpire or official for basketball, Little League and Colt baseball and softball. I watched a fellow referee get assaulted by an irate parent after a game, witnessed fights and observed both good and bad examples of sportsmanship. I have seen excellent coaches and ones that were not qualified, and as a college and high school coach for 26 years, I believe that I have the experience to appreciate the difference. Youth Sport has been a major part of my life and the lives of my children, and it has been an area of interest and concern for over 20 years. I began my formal research in the area of legal issues in youth sport in the spring of 1982, the same spring that Joey Fort was injured. I believe that this book can benefit parents, coaches, officials, and administrators who are involved in the youth sport experience. The purpose is to educate and inform, not to scare or tear down. Our children deserve the best sporting experience that we can provide, and it takes knowledge to do that.

Beginning with my experience as an instructor and counselor at Camp Winaukee in Center Harbor, New Hampshire in the summer of 1971, my work with the Clinton, South Carolina YMCA, coaching football, basketball, track, and golf on the interscholastic level, and football, basketball, and tennis on the collegiate level, I have been involved in sport and athletic competition for 28 years. I have experienced the great excitement of victory and the devastation of loss, but for 28 years I have been blessed.

There is an old story about a bridge builder that relates to the message of this book.

The Bridge Builder
Will Allen Dromgoole

An old man, going a lone highway,
Came, at the evening, cold and gray,
To a chasm, vast and deep, and wide,
Through which was flowing a sullen tide.
The old man crossed in the twilight dim;
The sullen stream had no fears for him;

But he turned, when safe on the other side,
And built a bridge to span the tide.
"Old man," said a fellow pilgrim, near,
"You are wasting strength with building here;
Your journey will end with the ending day;
You never again must pass this way;
You have crossed the chasm, deep and wide-
Why build you the bridge at the eventide?"
The builder lifted his old gray head;
"Good friend, in the path I have come," he said,
"There followeth after me today
A youth, whose feet must pass this way.
This chasm, that has been naught to me,
To that fair-haired youth may a pitfall be.
He, too, must cross in the twilight dim;
Good friend, I am building the bridge for him."

It is the aim of this book to build a safer and better bridge for generations of future participants in Youth Sport.

Contributing Authors

Gil B. Fried, Esq. is an Associate Professor at the University of New Haven's School of Business, teaching sports law, finance and facility management. Fried received his Master's Degree in Sport Administration and Juris Doctor from Ohio State University. Prior to joining the University of Houston faculty, Fried was the director of a San Francisco based Sports Law Center.

Dr. Stan Grosshandler is a member of the Raleigh Pain Clinic and Clinical Associate Professor of Anesthesiology at the University of North Carolina, Chapel Hill, North Carolina. He is an authority on sports history and author of numerous publications on that subject.

Dr. Gerald Hawkins is Professor of Exercise Studies and Director of Sports Medicine at Lander University, Greenwood, South Carolina. A Fellow in the American College of Sports Medicine, a National Athletic Trainers Association Certified Athletic Trainer, and a South Carolina Certified Athletic Trainer, he has had numerous international sports medicine appointments including the Junior League World Championships and Goodwill Games. He is author of numerous publications on sports medicine, physical fitness and exercise science. In 1999 Dr. Hawkins received the Governor's Award for Professor of the Year for South Carolina.

Index